MONEY $ENSE
for Kids!

by Hollis Page Harman, P.F.P.

BARRON'S

ACKNOWLEDGMENTS

My forefathers were consecrated to a vision of American education. In 1871, they founded what is known today as The Loomis Chaffee School in Windsor, Connecticut. As a daughter of the house of Loomis, it is fitting to acknowledge and continue their mission. Thank you, Barron's, for aiding and abetting a family vision.

First edition published 1999 by Barron's Educational Series, Inc.

© Text copyright 1999 by Hollis Page Harman

Design and illustrations © Copyright 1999

by Barron's Educational Series, Inc.

All inquiries should be addressed to:

Barron's Educational Series, Inc.

250 Wireless Boulevard

Hauppauge, New York 11788

http://www.barronseduc.com

International Standard Book No.: 0-7641-0681-3

Library of Congress Catalog Card No.: 98-27099

Library of Congress Cataloging-in-Publication Data

Harman, Hollis Page.

Money $ense for kids / by Hollis Page Harman.

p.   cm.

Includes bibliographical references (p.   ) and index.

Explains the nature of money, the different ways in which it can be represented and how it can be saved or invested, discussing mutual funds, the stock market, banks, and inflation. Includes games and activities.

ISBN 0-7641-0681-3

1. Money—Juvenile literature. 2. Saving and investment—Juvenile literature. 3. Finance, personal—Juvenile literature. [1. Money. 2. Saving and investment. 3. Finance, Personal.] I. Title.

HG221.5.H33 1999

332.024—dc2l   98-27099

                                                                                                          CIP

                                                                                                          AC

Printed in Hong Kong

98765432

TABLE OF CONTENTS

PART ONE SEE IT

PART TWO ADD TO IT

PART THREE GROW IT

PART FOUR FUN WITH IT

APPENDICES

DEDICATION

To the young and the old
modern and old fashioned
enlightened and in the dark.
It's never too late to lift life's lid.
I wish you all many lucky pennies
and the ability to explore life beyond the lid.

This book was a compelling inspiration.
I dedicate it to

Max and Zoë
Mom and Dad
Reed, Nan
Hayden, Spencer
And a power greater than us all.

THIS MONEY $ENSE FOR KIDS BOOK

BELONGS TO _____

PART ONE

See It

NOW | SHORT TERM | LONG TERM

PART ONE

SEE IT

Introduction

Dear kids, old souls, and bright angels,

I have a story to tell you. It's a true story. I believe in magic in my life and in everyone's lives. So I'll get you started.

$ Pick a coin or a bill you may already have or ask your mom and dad to give you one for this special project. They may want to lend it to you . . . that's okay, too.

$ Make your coin or bill special so it stands out next to the others. If you've picked a coin, you might paint half of it with your mom's colored nail polish. If you've picked a bill, you might put a paper clip on it.

$ Does it look different from the rest? Great.

This coin or bill is different; it's magical. Put it away in a very safe place.

$ Stick it in a clear jar with a lid, like a tomato sauce or peanut butter jar.

$ Label the jar LONG-TERM and put the lid on tightly .

$ Then kind of forget about it. Since it's in a clear jar, you can see it when you walk by. You can admire it. You can talk to it, say "hi." Leave it there; it's busy being magical.

Now that your special coin or bill is safe and sound, let's talk about money. The more you know about it, the easier it will be to find. Your specially decorated money wants a friend. How can you find the next coin or bill to keep this money company? And the next!

Read on: It's magic.

P.S. At the end of each chapter there will be a "TO DO" activity for you. Each completed activity will put you one step closer to having your very own magic money. Do them all.

MY TO DO LIST
Pick a coin or a bill.
Decorate it so it stands out from the others.
Label a clear jar LONG-TERM.
Put your money inside and close the lid.

CHAPTER ONE

Money

What is money? Why do we need it? How do we get it? What do we do with it? What do you ask your parents for? What do you want or need that they won't buy for you? What do you want or need that they can't buy for you?

Have you made *your wish list*? Good. Read this book and follow the steps. Do something from this book each day. You're young. You've got time. Money adds up. With the right choices, you may have as much as you need and want, plus more. However, if you decide you have no needs and wants, you can give your dimes and dollars to someone who does.

The Money Circle

Let's make it simple. Follow a dollar today and watch where the same dollar goes.

- $ You're lucky enough to have a dollar burning a hole in your pocket.
- $ You go to your favorite trading card store and buy baseball cards with the dollar.
- $ The young sales clerk from the trading card store uses the dollar to buy an ice cream cone.
- $ The ice cream vendor goes to the drugstore to buy a pack of chewing gum.

The dollar keeps changing hands, over and over until it wears out. Money moves in a big circle, from buyer to seller to another buyer, and on and on. In banks and electronic accounts, it moves from one account to another.

It's a Law

Congress passed into law the dollar money system in 1792. If you want to see where Congress was granted this power, open an encyclopedia to the United States Constitution. After the Preamble, "We the people," which you may have had to memorize in school, find

$ Article I, The Legislative Department, then find
$ Section 8, Powers Vested in Congress, then find
$ Part 5, "The Congress shall have power: . . . To coin money . . ."

At first, our currency was gold and silver dollars. After the Civil War, the government issued paper money. Finally, in 1913, Congress established a central banking system, the **Federal Reserve System,** often known as the Fed. The Fed's job is to regulate the supply of money so that the country can grow economically.

In the United States, our money is made up of bills and coins. We have seven different bills worth various amounts. All are the same size. We have five coins, each with a different value and size. Coins last much, much longer than bills because they are made of metal. You might get a penny that's 100 years old as change from the store, but you'll never get a dollar bill that old. Look at the dates on your change the next time you go to the store.

Old Money, New Money

Bills are made of special paper, and they wear out moving from wallet to pocket, cash register to bank, and back again. The Fed keeps track of how long bills usually last. Here's their report: The

$1 lasts about 18 months; the $5 lasts about 15 months; the $10 lasts about 18 months; the $20 lasts two years; the $50 lasts about five years; and the $100, eight and a half years. When bills wear out, our banks exchange them for new ones.

The bank sends them back to the Treasury Department, which burns them, millions of old dollars every day. Their ashes are packaged as bricks and used as roofing material or sold as insulation. Your roof could be made of money, and the insulation in your walls keeping you toasty could once have been wrinkled, old money.

MY TO DO LIST
Make a wish list
and a need list.

CHAPTER TWO
Bills

Each bill is incredibly beautiful and tells two different and important stories from American history. The first is the story of the man whose portrait is on the bill's face. The second is about the famous buildings, monuments, and paintings on the reverse side of the bills.

Before I tell those stories, I'll tell a third, one that all bills share. It's the story of the meaning of the numbers, letters, and symbols on all paper money in the United States. Find a magnifying glass. You can use it to get close up to the details I will explain.

If All Bills Could Talk

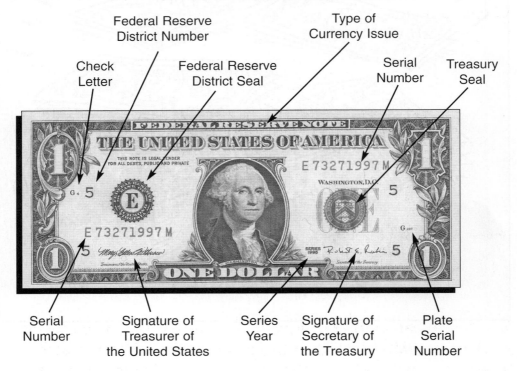

Federal Reserve District Number

Type of Currency Issue

Check Letter

Federal Reserve District Seal

Serial Number

Treasury Seal

Serial Number

Signature of Treasurer of the United States

Series Year

Signature of Secretary of the Treasury

Plate Serial Number

Diagram of $1 Bill

Place a $1 bill face up in front of you. Notice the color: black. Compare yours to the one in the picture. Feel the bill. The paper is made of linen and cotton with red and blue fibers woven through it. A special ink is made from a secret formula so that nobody can use it to print false, or counterfeit, money. Did you know that counterfeiters can be punished by going to jail for up to 15 years? Now look for the red and blue fibers in Washington's face? He almost looks tattooed.

Where Do They Come From?

Our bills are printed from a numbered engraving plate containing eight rows and four columns. Each sheet of paper has 32 bills printed on it. Find the tiny G4 on the left and the G397 on the right. The G4 tells us that before the sheet was cut apart, this bill was located on row G, column 4. The G397 tells us which engraving plate printed our bill.

Printing Plate with Bill Location

Know the Code

Now, by looking at a special code, we can find out where in the country our bill was shipped to before it reached its first bank. Look at the round seal on the left. This is the **Federal Reserve**

Seal that distinguishes the 12 districts of the **Federal Reserve System.** Each district has its own letter and corresponding number. The seal has this letter in its center. This same letter also precedes the green serial numbers appearing on the upper right and lower left sides of the bill. The corresponding number appears four times in black on the front of the note—two on each side, above and below the center. The seal on the bill in the picture has 5 and E. These stand for the Federal Reserve Richmond district. The map below shows the code for each district.

In our newly redesigned currency, the bills have a universal Federal Reserve Seal. The letter and number that identify the Federal Reserve district now appear under the left serial number.

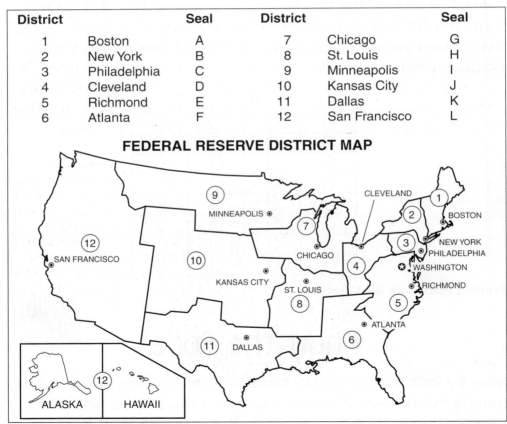

District		Seal	District		Seal
1	Boston	A	7	Chicago	G
2	New York	B	8	St. Louis	H
3	Philadelphia	C	9	Minneapolis	I
4	Cleveland	D	10	Kansas City	J
5	Richmond	E	11	Dallas	K
6	Atlanta	F	12	San Francisco	L

FEDERAL RESERVE DISTRICT MAP

Federal Reserve District Map

Serial Number

The **serial number** on older currency appears twice in green on the face of the bill, on the lower left and the upper right. On newer currency, it appears on the upper left and lower right. Each bill has a different serial number. No two bills will ever have the same serial number. Each bill has a serial number with eight numbers and a prefix and suffix letter. The prefix letter, as we just learned, identifies the Federal Reserve district. The suffix letter corresponds to a particular group of numbered bills. In newer currency, an additional letter has been added.

Treasury Department Seal

The round seal on the right is a symbol for the **Treasury Department**. This department is in charge of all our money. It tells the Bureau of Engraving and Printing (which is part of the department) how many bills to print and the U.S. Mint (another part of the department) how many coins to manufacture.

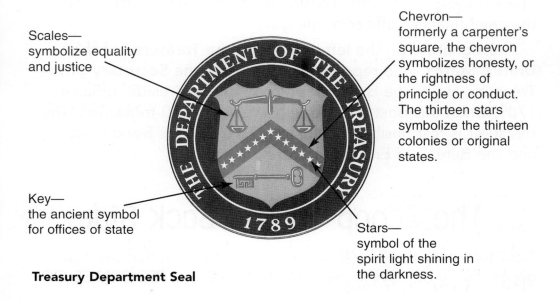

Scales—
symbolize equality and justice

Chevron—
formerly a carpenter's square, the chevron symbolizes honesty, or the rightness of principle or conduct. The thirteen stars symbolize the thirteen colonies or original states.

Key—
the ancient symbol for offices of state

Stars—
symbol of the spirit light shining in the darkness.

Treasury Department Seal

Within the round seal are several symbols. See the angled bar in the middle? It's called a chevron. The 13 stars within it represent the original states. The old-fashioned key below the chevron stands for the official authority of each state's government. The scales above are the scales of justice. They're balanced, to show that the United States has equal justice for all people. The wide band inside the circle says, "Department of the Treasury," and the year it was founded, 1789. It's interesting, isn't it? The Treasury Department collects taxes, prints postage stamps, forms banks, chooses designs for money, and has many other jobs as well.

Who Wrote on Our Bills

Two people sign all bills. Find the two cursive signatures. The one on the right belongs to the **Secretary of the Treasury**, who is appointed by the president and is a member of the cabinet. Since 1789, 70 people have served as Secretary of the Treasury. This person has one of the most important jobs in our government. The secretary advises the president on all money matters and is the chief financial officer of the government.

The signature on the left belongs to the **Treasurer of the United States**, who reports to and advises the **Secretary of the Treasury**. He or she is also appointed by the president. Since 1789, when this post was created, we've had 40 treasurers. The treasurer is responsible for the Mint, the Savings Bond Division, and the Bureau of Engraving and Printing.

The Scoop on the Back Side

Now turn over the $1 bill to the reverse side. Notice the color—green. Every bill says in capital letters THE UNITED STATES OF

AMERICA. Since 1963, every bill also has the legend, IN GOD WE TRUST, which is our national motto. Can you find them in the diagram that follows?

Back of Great Seal of the United States

Front of Great Seal of the United States

Plate Serial Number

Reverse Side of $1 Bill

The Broken Code

Let's review the story told on all bills. The Treasury Department, run by the secretary of the treasury, takes care of our country's money supply. The secretary gets help from the treasurer. Our country is divided into districts that distribute the money printed by the Bureau of Engraving and Printing. Each bill has its own number and is printed with special ink on a certain kind of paper to prevent counterfeiting.

Now we come to the other two stories from American history shown on each bill.

1. The story behind the portrait on the face of each bill is one terrific biography.
2. The picture on the reverse side is of a famous building, symbol, or event.

Bill Descriptions

BILL	FRONT	REVERSE
One	George Washington	Great Seal of the U.S.
Two	Thomas Jefferson	Declaration of Independence
Five	Abraham Lincoln	Lincoln Memorial
Ten	Alexander Hamilton	U.S. Treasury Building
Twenty	Andrew Jackson	White House
Fifty	Ulysses S. Grant	U.S. Capitol
One hundred	Benjamin Franklin	Independence Hall

The One-Dollar Bill

Who's on the face of the $1 bill? George Washington, our first president. The portrait was engraved on a printing plate by George Smillie, who copied a famous painting by Gilbert Stuart. This painting is owned by the National Portrait Gallery in Washington, D.C. and the Museum of Fine Arts in Boston, Massachusetts. It moves between these two locations every three years.

See if you can find the number 1 and the word one 16 times on the face and the back of a $1 bill. Hint: it appears six times on the face.

GEORGE WASHINGTON

Washington served two terms as president, starting in 1789. He was a great general in the American Revolution and was much loved by Americans. As our first president, Washington had the very hard task of taking 13 states and turning them into a united nation. He succeeded and has often been called the "father of our country."

Face of $1 Bill

The Great Seal

Turn the bill over to the reverse side. What you see is both sides of the **Great Seal**. The seal is also on the hats of members of the Army and the Air Force. The face is used to stamp official documents. The symbols on the seal stand for the branches of government and for the ideals on which the United States was founded.

Front and Reverse of Great Seal

At the center of the seal is the American bald eagle, with its claws and wings outstretched. The eagle's head stands for the executive branch. The shield, with 13 stripes, symbolizes the United States and the bar across the top of the shield represents Congress, or the legislative branch. The nine feathers in the tail represent the nine justices (judges) of the Supreme Court, or the judicial branch. The olive branch in the eagle's right claw has 13 leaves representing peace, and there are 13 arrows in the left claw symbolizing war. Which claw is the eagle looking toward? It looks toward the 13 leaves symbolizing peace. A ribbon held in the eagle's beak has a 13-letter Latin phrase, *E Pluribus Unum*. It means "One, Out of Many": one nation out of many states. It represents the promise that if people unite under democracy, they can build a great nation, and they did—the United States of America. Above the eagle's head are shimmering stars in a circle of darkness surrounded by a burst of light. This symbolizes the divine guidance that inspired the American Constitution.

The reverse side of the **Great Seal** depicts an unfinished pyramid topped by a triangle with an eye inside. The pyramid symbolizes strength and endurance. The unfinished state of the pyramid represents our nation's continuing growth and improvement. The eye represents the "All-seeing Eye" of God. Two important Latin mottos decorate the seal. The first, near the "All-seeing Eye," is *Annuit Coeptis* which means "God Blesses our Undertakings." Below is the motto, *Novus Ordo Seclorum*, which means "New Order of the Ages." Directly above are the Roman numerals MDCCLXXVI (1776).

If you visit Washington, D.C., you can see both sides of the Great Seal in the main building of the Department of State. It is displayed in the great hall that holds flags from many nations, where visiting heads of state enter the building.

The Two-Dollar Bill

My favorite paper money is the $2 bill, Series 1976 and 1996. It's the only bill with people on the reverse side. Prior to 1976, an illustration of Monticello, Jefferson's home, was pictured.

THOMAS JEFFERSON

Face of $2 Bill

On the face of the bill is a portrait of Thomas Jefferson, who served as our third president, from 1801 to 1809. Jefferson was a remarkable statesman and a man of many talents and interests. He was secretary of state, vice president, and later, president. He was an architect who designed buildings and gardens, and an inventor (he invented the dumbwaiter, a tiny elevator to bring food to the dining room). His personal collection of books became the Library of Congress. Jefferson compiled his own Bible, and he played the violin. He was the first American to put forth the idea that all Americans should get a free, public education. Although he didn't achieve that goal, he did found the University of Virginia.

Jefferson's most important contribution to American history was writing the first draft of the Declaration of Independence, the signing of which is pictured on the reverse side of the $2 bill. What Jefferson wrote became the foundation of America's form of government: ". . . all men are created equal, that they are endowed . . . with certain unalienable rights, that among these rights are Life, Liberty and the pursuit of Happiness . . . ."

THE DECLARATION OF INDEPENDENCE

Reverse Side of $2 Bill

The engraving on the reverse side of the $2 bill is based on the famous John Trumbull painting, *The Signing of the Declaration of Independence.* The bill was printed in 1996 in honor of the 200th anniversary of the signing of the Declaration of Independence on July 4, 1776. It was reissued in 1996 with Robert Rubin's signature as secretary of the treasury and Mary Ellen Withrow's signature as treasurer. The engraving shows John Hancock seated on the right, with John Adams, Roger Sherman, Robert Livingston, Thomas Jefferson, and Benjamin Franklin standing to the left.

The Five-Dollar Bill

THE OLD FIVE
Honest Abe

Face of Old $5 Bill

"Honest Abe," the nickname of our sixteenth president, appears on the face of the $5 bill. Abraham Lincoln was a man who truly started out with nothing, living in a humble cabin in Illinois. But think about how amazing this was—that a man who came from that world was able to become president of the United States.

Lincoln was president during the Civil War, when the southern states left the union over the issue of slavery. Lincoln issued the Emancipation Proclamation that freed the slaves. In his famous Gettysburg Address, Lincoln is remembered for these words: ". . . a government of the people, by the people, for the people, shall not perish from the earth." He delivered this speech at the dedication of the National Cemetery in Gettysburg, where the Union soldiers who had died in that battle were laid to rest. Only one year after the war ended, he was assassinated by John

Wilkes Booth while watching a play at Ford's Theater in Washington, D.C.

The Lincoln Memorial

Reverse Side of Old $5 Bill

On the reverse side of the $5 bill is an engraving of the Lincoln Memorial, in Washington, D.C. If you look closely, you can see a statue of Lincoln seated between two columns in the middle of the building. The Gettysburg Address and his second inaugural speech are engraved on the memorial's walls. The 36 columns around the outside of the building stand for the number of states in 1865, the year the Civil War ended. Martin Luther King Jr. chose the steps of the Lincoln Memorial to deliver his famous "I Have a Dream" speech in 1963. Like the Gettysburg Address, this speech reminds us of the equality of all Americans, whatever their color.

THE NEW FIVE

Face and Reverse Sides of New $5 Bill

The $5 bill was redesigned in 2000. Unlike many of the other new bills, it has no color shifting ink. The security thread, located to the left of Lincoln's portrait, glows blue in ultraviolet light. The thread reads "USA FIVE" and a flag with the number "5" in the star field can be seen from both sides.

The Ten-Dollar Bill

THE OLD TEN

Alexander Hamilton

Face of Old $10 Bill

Alexander Hamilton's portrait is on the face of the $10 bill. He was not a president of the United States; he was a Revolutionary War hero who was appointed the first U.S. treasury secretary under George Washington. Hamilton proposed the creation of a mint to coin money and a national bank to help manage America's economy. Thomas Jefferson (on the face of the $2 bill) thought that such a bank was unconstitutional. After much arguing, the Supreme Court finally agreed with Hamilton. This argument was one of several issues that led to the formation of the first political parties in America. The Federalists, backed by Hamilton, believed in a strong central government. The Democratic-Republicans, backed by Jefferson, believed that the states and its citizens should have more power than the central government.

Hamilton is also remembered for writing *The Federalist Papers*. He wrote them to explain our proposed Constitution to the people of New York state. Hamilton hoped that his explanation would convince New Yorkers to approve the Constitution. In *The Federalist Papers*, Hamilton wrote of a government with the same laws for the rich and the poor. He described a system of checks and balances among the executive, legislative, and judicial branches of government. These checks and balances would prevent any one branch from becoming more powerful than the others. Hamilton made his case, and the New York vote ratified the Constitution.

U.S. Treasury

Reverse Side of Old $10 Bill

On the reverse side of the bill is the U.S. Treasury building, which is located next to the White House. Built in 1836, it is the oldest government building in Washington, D.C. In 1997, the Treasury Department and its bureaus employed approximately 157,000 full-time employees. It had authority over an estimated budget of $371.4 billion.

THE NEW TEN

Face and Reverse Sides of New $10 Bill

The new $10 bill was also issued in 2000. On the new $10, however, the security thread is to the right of the portrait. Under ultraviolet light, the thread glows orange, reads "USA TEN," and has the number "10" in the star field of the flag. Find the number "10" on the front of the note in the lower right corner and watch the color shift from green to black.

The Twenty-Dollar Bill

THE OLD TWENTY
Old Hickory

Face of Old $20 Bill

Andrew Jackson, our seventh president, is on the face of the $20 bill. Jackson was a lawyer by profession and a fighter throughout his life. A man with an iron will, he was nicknamed "Old Hickory" after the tough hardwood tree. Look at his portrait. When I do, I see a man whose smile turns down. Historians say he was a man who loved the common people and was loved by them, but the rich didn't like him because of his policies on money.

During Jackson's presidency, from 1829 to 1837, the West and other parts of the country were being settled. When the state of Georgia wanted to kick the Cherokee Indians off their land, the U.S. Supreme Court ruled against Georgia. But Jackson refused to enforce the Court's decision by sending troops to Georgia. The Cherokee left their land and went West, a journey now remembered as the "Trail of Tears." Jackson and others genuinely believed that they were moving the Indians to better lands. However, many people disagreed with him then, and today his decision seems cruel and unfair. Yet he is credited with the great western expansion of our country during his presidency.

The White House

Reverse Side of Old $20 Bill

On the reverse side of the $20 bill is an engraving of the White House, where the president lives and works. It was designed by architect James Hoban. It was first called the President's Palace, but its name changed from "Palace" to "House" to emphasize that the United States had an elected president rather than a king. In 1800, John Adams, our second president, became the first president to live there. The British burned the White House during the War of 1812, and it has been remodeled several times since.

The White House sits on 18 acres of green space, full of trees, shrubs, flowers, and fountains. The house itself has three stories and a two-story basement. The interior is made up of 132 rooms, plus 32 bathrooms. It has 147 windows, 412 doors, seven staircases, three elevators, and 12 chimneys. Many of the rooms are named for their colors. The Red Room has red satin walls, and the walls of the Green Room were originally covered with green silk.

The president and his family live in a private apartment on the second floor, which also has several guest rooms. The third floor has 15 bedrooms, a small kitchen, a solarium, and a playroom. The basement is two stories deep and has a bomb shelter. In the wings of the main building are a swimming pool, gymnasium, and theater.

Imagine what it would be like to live there? Think about all the history that has taken place in the White House. Think what it must be like for all the children who have lived there. Can you see yourself walking the dog on the great lawn and catching your favorite television show in the Oval Office?

THE NEW TWENTY

Face and Reverse Sides of New $20 Bill

In the fall of 1998, the third U.S. bill was redesigned. The new $20 is unique because it can be machine-read by the blind. Like the new $50, it has a large dark numeral in a light background on the back of the note that makes it easier to identify. The security thread on the new $20 is now located to the far left and appears green when held up to ultraviolet light. Other security features are similar to the new $50 and $100 bills described later. The old $20s will continue to be recirculated. The old $50s and $100s will be replaced with the new designs. For some reason, the old $20 note has been the most frequently counterfeited bill in our country.

The Fifty–Dollar Bill

THE OLD FIFTY
Ulysses S. Grant

Face of Old $50 Bill

Ulysses S. Grant, whose face is on the $50 bill, was our eighteenth president, from 1869 to 1877. President Lincoln made Grant general in chief of the Union Army during the Civil War. It was Grant's strategy that won the war for the Union. He was widely admired as a soldier and became a national hero. Grant's popularity, energy, and determination won him the election held after Lincoln was assassinated.

Unfortunately, Grant turned out to be a better general than president. Some important events occurred during his time in office—Yellowstone became our first national park, the National Baseball League was organized, the first transcontinental railroad was completed, and Alexander Graham Bell invented the telephone. In 1870, the states ratified the Fifteenth Amendment to the Constitution, which gave African American men the right to vote.

Grant, however, was a poor judge of character. He placed his trust in people who stole from and corrupted the government. He said, "It was my fortune, or misfortune to be called to the office of Chief Executive without any previous political training. Mistakes have been made as all can see and I admit." Still, the American people elected him to a second term in office.

The Capitol

Reverse Side of Old $50 Bill

On the reverse side of the $50 bill is a picture of the Capitol building, which contains the Senate and the House of Representatives. Here laws are made—protecting civil rights, providing medical care for the poor and elderly, and levying taxes on the population. Each state elects two senators (100 senators in all) and one representative for about 588,000 people (435 representatives in all).

The Capitol building is five stories tall and covers $3\frac{1}{2}$ acres. It is known for its huge white dome with a $19\frac{1}{2}$-foot bronze statue, *Freedom*, on top. It was designed by William Thornton in 1793 and completed in 1850. The Great Rotunda inside the front entrance contains a gallery of famous Revolutionary War paintings.

THE NEW FIFTY

The new $50 bill was issued in 1997. It has three very nifty features. Look at the reverse side of the bill. What stands out?

Face and Reverse Sides of the New $50 Bill

The big number 50 on the lower right-hand side. This is a new low-vision feature that was introduced for the first time on the $50. The security thread is on the right side of the bill. In ultraviolet light, the security thread will turn yellow, not green like the $20. Do you remember where the security thread is located on the $20?

The One-Hundred-Dollar Bill

THE OLD BEN

Now let's look at a $100 bill. You may as well get used to looking at these because you'll have a lot of them one day if you save. It's a "big" bill because it's worth a lot—a tall pile of $1 bills—but the paper itself is physically the same size as all the other bills.

Benjamin Franklin

Benjamin Franklin is on the face of the $100 bill. (He is on the back of the $2 bill, also, among the men signing the Declaration of Independence.) He coined the famous saying, "Money makes money and the money that money makes makes more money."

Face of Old $100 Bill

Franklin knew what he was talking about. He was a very good businessman. He is remembered as a wise national leader with many talents and skills. He was a printer first, then began writing and printing his writings. He published a newspaper that was the first to use cartoons and maps to illustrate stories. He also wrote and published *Poor Richard's Almanac*, where he gave advice sprinkled with his own witty sayings. Franklin is still quoted today. He's the one who said, "Early to bed, early to rise, makes a man healthy, wealthy, and wise." Franklin was also a scientist and an inventor. He invented bifocal eyeglasses and helped found the University of Pennsylvania in Philadelphia.

When we think of Benjamin Franklin, though, what we usually think of is the part he played in the country's early history. He signed four of America's most important historical documents: the Declaration of Independence, the Treaty of Alliance with France, The Treaty of Peace with Great Britain, and the Constitution of the United States. He also served his country in public office and as a diplomat.

Independence Hall

Reverse Side of Old $100 Bill

On the reverse side of the $100 bill is a picture of Independence Hall, or the Old State House, in Philadelphia, a building Benjamin Franklin knew well. The Declaration of Independence was signed here on July 4, 1776. The Liberty Bell hung in the tower, and was rung on July 8, 1776 to announce the reading of the signed Declaration of Independence. Look carefully at the clock below the tower. What time is it? Use a magnifying glass to answer this question. It looks like 4:10 to me.

THE NEW BEN

In 1996 the $100 bill was given a new design. Compare the new design to the old. The portrait of Franklin is much larger and more detailed on the new bills. It's not centered, either—if you put an old bill on top of a new one, you can see that the portraits don't line up. Then look to the right of the portrait and find the new watermark of Franklin. Around his coat is a very small line that says "The United States of America" over and over. These features were included to prevent counterfeiting. Let's look at some of the other changes many of the new bills have in common.

Face of New $100 Bill

Reverse Side of New $100 Bill

$ Look at the number 100 in the lower left corner. "USA 100" is printed over and over in tiny little letters within the number.

$ Check for the 100 in the lower right-hand corner. When you look at it straight on, it looks green. Viewed from an angle, it changes color and looks black. These new bills have color-shifting ink.

$ Find the security thread that can be seen from both sides and that reads "USA 100." It's on the left side of the bill. In ultraviolet light the thread will turn red. That's how you know it's not counterfeit. Do you remember the colors of the other security threads? Where are they located on each of the new bills?

$ Find the Federal Reserve seal. It's now a general seal for all the districts. To find which branch of the Federal Reserve Bank issued the note, look for the letter and number below the serial number.

$ Count the letters and numbers in the serial number. The number now has 11 in all—an extra letter was added to the prefix.

Now you know the stories that go with each of our seven bills. You can tell those stories to other people. You can make the bill come alive for your listeners, and they will tell the bill's story to other friends. On and on it will go.

MY TO DO LIST

Tell at least one person the story on the $1 bill.

CHAPTER THREE
Coins

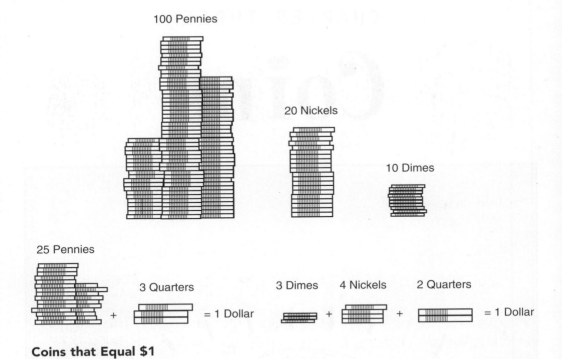

100 Pennies

20 Nickels

10 Dimes

25 Pennies

3 Quarters + = 1 Dollar

3 Dimes + 4 Nickels + 2 Quarters = 1 Dollar

Coins that Equal $1

What do you use coins for? You use coins to make change for dollar bills. You probably need coins to use a pay phone and maybe to get a drink from a vending machine or to buy milk in the school cafeteria. We may use coins every day, but we probably don't look at them closely very often. There's one coin where the head faces right. Without looking at your money, do you know which coin it is? It's the Lincoln penny.

Our Five Coins

Name the Presidents on Coins

Let's look at the coins in common circulation today. They are: pennies, nickels, dimes, quarters, and half-dollars. The front of the coins shows only portraits of U.S. presidents, who were selected by Congress and the Department of the Treasury to honor their contribution to our country. The reverse side of the coins shows buildings, seals, or symbols, just like bills.

$ The Lincoln penny was issued in 1909 to commemorate the 100th anniversary of Abraham Lincoln's date of birth. On the back is an imprint of the Lincoln Memorial.

$ In 1938, 390 artists competed for the honor of designing the nickel. Thomas Jefferson's portrait was selected for the face and his historic home in Virginia, Monticello, was chosen to be featured on the reverse side.

$ Less than a year after Franklin D. Roosevelt's death, on what would have been his birthday, January 30, 1946, the dime with his likeness on the front was issued. He served as president for four terms, longer than any other man. The back of the dime carries the liberty torch with olive and oak branches symbolizing victory and strength. This is the same torch held by the Statue of Liberty.

$ George Washington's portrait was selected for the face of the quarter to commemorate his 200th birthday. The reverse side depicts the bald eagle—our national bird since 1782.

$ After John F. Kennedy's assassination, President Lyndon Johnson authorized the Treasury Department to mint the 50-cent piece with Kennedy's image. He was our youngest president. On the back of the coin is the Presidential Coat of Arms.

Coin Descriptions

COIN	FRONT	REVERSE
Penny . . . $.01 Lincoln Cent	Abraham Lincoln	Lincoln Memorial
Nickel . . . $.05 Jefferson Nickel	Thomas Jefferson	Monticello (Jefferson's home)
Dime . . . $.10 Roosevelt Dime	Franklin D. Roosevelt	Torch with olive and oak branch
Quarter . . . $.25 Washington Quarter	George Washington	Bald Eagle
Half Dollar . . . $.50 Kennedy Half-Dollar	John F. Kennedy	Presidential Coat of Arms
One Dollar Coin	Dwight D. Eisenhower	Bald Eagle
One Dollar Coin	Susan B. Anthony	Bald Eagle
One Dollar Coin	Sacagawea	Bald Eagle

DOLLAR COINS

Dollar coins have had an interesting history. The Dwight D. Eisenhower dollar coin was replaced in 1979 by the Susan B. Anthony dollar coin, which hasn't been minted since 1981 and is no longer in general circulation. It honors the famous women's rights leader (1820–1906) who helped women get the right to vote. In 1920, the Nineteenth Amendment granted women the right to vote. I have gotten Susan B. Anthony dollars as change from the stamp machine at the post office. If you find one, hang onto it; keep it for *your* kids.

The Golden Dollar Coin

Face and Reverse of Golden Dollar Coin

The Golden Dollar Coin, issued in 2000, depicts Sacagawea and her infant son, John-Baptiste. Sacagawea was the Shoshone Indian guide who led the Lewis and Clark expedition through the Northwest in 1804. The coin has a smooth edge and an extra-wide border. This distinctive edge distinguishes it from the quarter. Did you know the edges on our various coins help blind people identify different denominations?

STATE QUARTERS

In 1999, new commemorative quarters were issued. The front of the quarter with George Washington stays the same. But the bald eagle on the reverse side flies away until 2009 to be replaced by 50 different images: one from each state, at ten-week intervals, in the order they joined the union.

Here is a preview of the first five states' designs.

1. Delaware has a Revolutionary War hero riding a galloping horse with the words "The First State."
2. Pennsylvania shows the mythical figure of the Commonwealth in an outline of the state's borders.
3. New Jersey shows a scene from the famous painting *Washington Crossing the Delaware,* by Emmanuel Leutze.
4. Connecticut honors a white oak in winter, which stands for the state's freedom from the British.
5. Georgia depicts the peach inside the state's boundaries, with the state motto, "Wisdom, Justice, Moderation."

In Massachusetts, the quarter's design became a contest among the elementary school students. In a February 1998 press release, Governor Paul Cellucci said, "Soon, kids from North Carolina to California will pull a coin out of their pockets and find a symbol of Massachusetts created by someone their own age. . . . This quarter will carry the pride of Massachusetts, our history, and our youth all across the country."

Each of the 50 coins will let us hold a fragment of significant state history in our hands. We may add 50 state stories to our knowledge of American history, as well as 50 different works of art to carry in our pockets.

SHOW AND TELL

These five phrases are stamped on every American coin. See if you can find each on your coins.

- $ "Liberty"
- $ "In God We Trust"
- $ "The United States of America"
- $ *E Pluribus Unum* (Latin for "One, Out of Many")
- $ Amount of the coin written out

Now let's look even more closely. You may need a magnifying glass for this next task. Find any nickel. Turn it "heads" side up. The president you see is Thomas Jefferson, who is also on the front of the $2 bill. Look under President Jefferson's collar, where the lower edge of his collar meets the rim of the coin. Do you see the capital letters "FS"? These are the initials of Felix Schlag. He's the medalist who carved Jefferson's head in 1938.

Now find a dime, our smallest coin. The president on the dime is Franklin Roosevelt, our thirty-second president, who was in office from 1932 to 1945. Follow President Roosevelt's chin down to the tip of his neck. Do you see the letters "JS" a little bit to the right? They're the initials of John R. Sinnock, who carved the head on the dime that was issued in 1946.

Some coins have a mint mark near the date. *D* means that the coin was produced at the Denver, Colorado, mint, *P* or no mint mark is the Philadelphia Mint, *S* is the San Francisco Mint, and *W* is the West Point Mint. The Denver and Philadelphia mints produce most of our coins for general circulation. The Denver Mint produces about 32 million coins of all denominations daily. The San Francisco Mint produces mainly commemorative coins that honor events, people, or places. They are the kind collectors buy for long-term profit. The West Point Mint produces some of our uncirculated investment-grade gold, silver, and platinum coins.

OLD COINS

Many years ago, my grandmother gave me a few silver dollars. When I found them recently, I looked at the dates and the mint marks. One was minted in 1921 with a *D* for the Denver mint. Just for fun, I looked it up in a coin book. I found I had a Morgan Silver Dollar, one of the only Morgan Silver Dollars struck from the Denver Mint. It was worth not $1 but $49!

Silver Dollar

If you know anyone with a lot of old coins, ask if you can look through them. You'll be surprised at what you will find. The very old ones will increase in value every year just as my grandmother's silver dollars did. Since coins are metal, they last a long, long time. In contrast, bills wear out. The older the coin, the more history it has. It can teach us about history, geography, and art. When we look at the date it was minted, we can ask ourselves these questions:

Could this very coin have been held by Andrew Jackson or Ulysses S. Grant? Could it have been in Lincoln's pocket when he delivered the Gettysburg Address? Or was it with Lewis and Clark when they left to explore the Northwest in 1803?

The answer is YES! If only these old coins could talk, imagine the stories they could tell. Some of these old coins are only found in collections or coin stores. The hobby of collecting coins is called numismatics. Here are some interesting examples of collectible coins.

"P" Nickel

"P" Nickel

After the Japanese attacked Pearl Harbor in 1941, our supply of nickel ran low because the government needed the metal to make war materials. So President Roosevelt told the U.S. Mint to make 5-cent coins from a mixture of silver and other metals. See if any of your nickels are dated 1942, 1943, 1944, or 1945. Then look at the reverse side of the coin and see if there's a "P" (for Philadelphia, where they were minted) under the Latin phrase *E Pluribus Unum*. If there is, you have one of the only silver nickels ever made in the United States.

Wheat Penny

Wheat Penny

The reverse side of the wheat penny has two wheat sheaves, one on either side. My daughter found three of these just by looking carefully. She didn't even use a magnifying glass. According to collectors, these are the most popular of all U.S. coins. They were last minted in 1958. Some coin dealers sell them by the pound, $20 per pound. I'll bet you can find some of these.

The Three-Legged Buffalo Nickel

Three-Legged Buffalo Nickel

In 1937, when the three-legged Buffalo nickels were minted, the die that stamped the buffalo got damaged. The man who was pressing the coins tried to fix the die and accidentally filed away one of the buffalo's legs. He kept stamping away because he had a deadline to meet. The coins went into circulation before anyone knew he had made a mistake. Today one of those coins is worth not 5 cents but $1,500 if it is in mint condition. See if you can find one of those.

Now you know what bills and coins look like. You can tell their stories to your friends and family. Ask them to find the engraver's initials on coins. Explain the plate number on each bill. Show them how beautiful each bill and coin is—a lot of people may not have taken the time to look.

MY TO DO LIST
Feel the different edges of my coins.
Collect all 50 new state quarters.

PART TWO

Add
to It

NOW

SHORT
TERM

LONG
TERM

CHAPTER FOUR
Find It

Yuu're one step ahead. You know what money looks like and how it feels. The next step is to have some of your very own. How can you add to the collection you started way back in the introduction? That money wants a friend.

$ Find it
$ Ask for it
$ Earn it
$ Do one or all three
$ But DO IT

Now that you know what currency looks like, you may notice that you find it when you least expect it. Like me, you may have passed it by. But now you pick it up and look at it. You may find it in the sofa cushions, near the curb, or on the sidewalk. Does it belong to someone? Ask. If not, you just got lucky. Some days you may find several coins and other days you may find none. But it's fun to think about walking out the door and seeing what you may find. Here are a couple of true stories about finding money.

The Lucky Penny

I ride my bike a lot. As I ride, I see coins on the pavement. I used to ride over them. Now I stop. I can't wait to see what I've found. Most of them are beat up pennies. Cars and trucks have driven over these coins, making them even more special to me. I think they're lucky. I keep them on a shelf in the kitchen with the coins I find in the wash. It's my collection of battered coins. If someone admires one of them, I show them what I know about it and give them the coin. Sometimes I find two pennies during my bike trip. That's really exciting. I give one away to someone I meet on the road. I pass the luck on to another person. It feels great.

The Nifty Fifty

One day I was at a big warehouse store with my son, Max, and my daughter, Zoë. We were shopping for a birthday present for a preschool friend. At that time, Max was six and Zoë was four and a half. Max, who was a few steps behind me, caught up to me. He was waving an open white envelope. Very happily and loudly, he announced, "Mommy, look what I found!" He then took out a bill and waved it around like the American flag on July 4. It was a $50 bill: a nifty fifty. Big bucks! I was as excited as Max, but because I'm older, I realized that this was "found money." Anyone could come up to Max and claim it. If you lost a $50 bill, wouldn't you want the person who found it to try to find you?

So we marched up to the customer service desk and told the man behind the counter that we'd found some money. He said, "Give it to me and I'll keep it in the safe until someone claims it." But I thought, "Who will get the money if no one claims it? The man behind the desk? But Max was the one who found it."

So I said, "Here's what we're prepared to do. I'll give you our phone number and if someone comes and says he has lost some money, he can call my son and tell him how much he lost. If it matches the amount he found, we'll be happy to give the money back. Otherwise, it's Max's money. There's a famous old saying, 'Finders keepers; losers weepers.'" Guess what. No one ever called. Max now had a nifty fifty of his very own.

CHAPTER FIVE

Ask for It

What if you don't find any coins for a few days? Another way to add to your growing coin collection is to ask for money. Here are a couple of ideas.

Allowances

If your family likes the idea of allowances, ask for a reasonable amount of money each week. Maybe that formula is your age times 25 cents, or your age times $1. Find a happy balance with your parents. They might want you to do a few things around the house in exchange for this allowance. They might just give it to you and suggest what you might buy with it.

In our home, an allowance is like a grown-up's paycheck. It's money I give Max and Zoë for doing a few jobs. I give them each three $1 bills a week. We keep a chart on our refrigerator. Max and Zoë alternate doing these chores. They look at the chart all the time to make sure they are even. And they refer to it to see whose turn it is to do a job next. They put their initials next to the jobs they have completed. The chart is helpful, and it's a foolproof reminder.

Allowance Chart

TO DO	S	M	T	W	TH	F	SA
Recycling							
Newspapers							
Trash							
Set table							
Clear table							

Three Magic Money Jars

The kids take their bills and put $1 each in three different clear jars with lids. One is called **NOW**, one is called **SHORT-TERM**, and one is called **LONG-TERM**. If you recall from the introduction, I suggested you put a special coin or bill in a clear jar with a lid labeled LONG-TERM. The jars keep your money organized while it's at home. Here's what each jar is for:

1. **NOW**—Take this money out any time and spend it on anything you need. Or want! Or better yet, share some of your money with someone less fortunate.
2. **SHORT-TERM**—This jar is for larger purchases. Don't spend this every week. Let the bills add up in here for a while and use them to buy a big item that you feel you want or think you need. It's hard to wait, I know. But you'll be glad you did.
3. **LONG-TERM**—The money in this jar goes directly into the bank. It is for savings only. **YOU MAY NOT SPEND THIS MONEY**. You'll make it grow and then you'll use it for big expenses or purchases in the future. Maybe you'll use it to help pay for college. Maybe you'll buy a car when you're old enough. Maybe you'll get someone you love the best present in the world.

Gifts

Here's another way to add to your jars. Every year you have a birthday. For a birthday present, ask your grandparents or your parents to give you some money for your long-term jar. There are also holidays during the year. You might want to put money on your list of gifts to receive. That will give your family a choice of what they decide to give you.

Remember, if you get an allowance, some of it will always go into your long-term jar. Some of what you ask for will also go into your long-term jar. Are you watching the jars get full? This is how you save. Add a little bit to each jar often. We'll talk later about ways to grow what you've saved.

Finding and asking for money are easy. But you still may end up with nothing. Keep looking and keep asking. However, one certain way to find that special coin or bill a friend is to earn it. If you do a job well for someone who will pay you, you will surely end up with money. The sooner you have some money, the sooner you can use it to make more. So whatever you decide—to wait for found money, to ask for money, or to earn it—just begin. **Do it now.**

MY TO DO LIST
Label two more clear jars: NOW and SHORT-TERM.

CHAPTER SIX

Earn It

Ask your family if you could earn money for your three jars by working around the house. Then ask them if you could ask your neighbors if you could do odd jobs for them. If they say yes, you're on your way to increasing your cash.

The next question is how to earn it. Discuss these next ideas with your parents in advance. Make sure they approve. After all, they have experience. They might have other ideas for you to try. They might say no to some of what's listed below. Put your ideas together and figure out how you can use them to make money. Maybe something you like to do or make is also something you can sell or charge people for.

Sell Something

Stuff to sell:

$ **Soda cans.** You can collect these and sell them to a company that recycles metal.

$ **Bottles.** Some states make buyers pay a deposit that they get back if they return the bottle. But lots of people throw the bottles out anyway. Collect them, return them to the store, and pocket the change.

$ **Outgrown clothes, books, and toys.** Make sure your parents agree with this idea. Have a garage sale of all the stuff you've outgrown. Ask your friends to bring over their outgrown items. Offer to sell items for your neighbors. Have a big sale. Check for rules about sale permits in your town.

$ **Collections.** Some of you may have collected baseball cards, Barbie dolls, virtual pets, and other toys. You'll have to do some homework to find out how much to charge.

$ **Stuff you make.** Do you love arts and crafts? Make pressed flower notecards, lanyards, recipe holders, or anything else you think someone might buy.

$ **Stuff you bake.** You can make birthday cakes, cookies, brownies, or chocolate sauce.

Do a Job

$ **Inside**
Water plants
Clean fish aquariums
Polish silver or furniture

$ **Outside**
Mow and trim lawns
Make deliveries for stores
Wash cars
Rake leaves

$ **For younger kids**
Babysit after school, nights or weekends
Be a study buddy or tutor
Coach sports or give lessons in sports

$ **For older adults**
Carry packages
Help with shopping
Run errands

Bring in the mail
Clean out the garage
Help with housework if they supervise you

$ **Using your talents and skills**
Bake birthday cakes, brownies, and cookies
Make pressed flower notecards
Create recipe holders made from clothespins

JOB SKILLS

After you decide how you want to make money, you have to fig-ure out how much to charge. Here are several ideas. Find out what the going rate is for the job. Ask someone who baby-sits, for example, how much to charge per hour. Another idea is to ask the person who needs the job done what the work is worth. Make sure the person knows how much time you will need to do the job well and explain exactly what you'll do. If you've done the job before, tell your new customer how much you got paid last time. Remember, for some jobs, experience counts. Going back to the baby-sitting example, you can charge more if you've done a lot of baby-sitting.

If you agree to do a job, make sure you arrive on time and do the job well. A responsible worker is a valuable worker. The per-son you are working for may want to tell others what a terrific worker you are. Do you know what that means? It may mean more jobs if you want them.

Let's say you've done such a good job that two different neighbors want you to work the same day. But you can't possibly be two places at one time. Plus each job will take a full day. What do you do? Here's one suggestion. Have a friend help you so you can do both jobs in one day. You will make twice as much money in the same amount of time. Then pay your friend for helping you.

Many adults started building their work skills when they were your age, doing the same jobs you can do now. They proved at an early age that they were dependable, organized, motivated, and willing to try. Here's a list of jobs grown-ups do and how much they are paid to do them.

Salaries Earned by Some Adults

School teacher—elementary	$37,900
Chief Executive of IBM (from '97 Annual Report)	$1,500,000
President of U.S.	$200,000
Vice President of U.S.	$171,500
Information scientist (I.S.)	$35,400
Police officer	$41,200
Bank teller	$16,300
Children's librarian	$34,600
Firefighter	$28,800

Median annual earnings for 1996, Occupational Outlook Handbook 1998–1999 edition.

Remember, when you come home with the money you've earned for a job well done, put some of the cash in each of your three jars.

MY TO DO LIST
Pick a job I could do now.

CHAPTER SEVEN

Risk It

Now that you've collected some bills and coins, you need to understand the magic of money. The magic of money isn't just having it sit there in a jar. The magic is making it grow. Over the long term, there are different ways to make it grow. I'll begin to explain them to you by comparing them to bikes. You need to know about the idea of *risk*, too. Risk means the chances you take. With both bikes and money, the faster you go, the greater the risk.

Bike Comparisons

There are lots of different kinds of bikes. Some are very easy to ride, and you probably won't fall off and hurt yourself. These bikes, though, won't take you very far or very fast. Others are harder to ride and go faster, but you have a greater chance of crashing.

Making your money grow is similar to riding a bike. Some ways of making it grow are easy and safe. You won't earn a lot of money, but you probably won't lose any. Other ways are riskier. You might earn a lot more money, but you may also lose it all.

When you were very small, you may have had a **baby bike.** It had a flat base, no wheels, and no pedals. It stayed in one place and rocked back and forth. You could belly flop on it and get a great safe ride.

Your long-term money is like that baby bike. As long as you keep the jar in a safe place, you're not going to lose any money. But the only way you can increase the amount of money in the jar is to put it there yourself.

Pretty soon after you learn to ride a baby bike you go on to a **tricycle.** The tricycle goes faster with less effort because the pedals do some of the work for you. But because you're going a little faster and are higher up, you could fall more easily.

Putting your money in a **savings account** is like riding a tricycle. You'll make more money because you'll earn **interest** (we'll talk more about interest, but basically it's money you get in exchange for letting someone borrow your money for a while). You won't lose any money either, because money you put in the bank is protected. But you won't make as much money as you would if you invested your money in something riskier.

After a while, you see the kid across the street riding a bike with only two wheels. Now that looks exciting, you think. So you get a **two-wheeler with training wheels** for stability and a bike helmet. Off you go. Now you can go faster. You have to watch where you're going because you're traveling further and faster. Maybe you're allowed to ride to the stop sign at the end of the block.

Buying **bonds** is like riding a two-wheeler with training wheels. We'll talk more about bonds, but basically a bond is another way to loan money and earn interest. With a bond, you'll probably earn more than you would with a savings account. But you can't be sure. There's a chance you could lose money, too.

After a few more trips to the stop sign, you decide you don't need training wheels anymore. So your parents undo the training wheels and off you go. This two-wheeler is a wobbly ride, but it's also very exciting. You pull back into the driveway having had the ride of your life. Now you know how your parents feel on their road bikes. You look forward to riding a bike with skinny tires and lots of gears and wearing shoes that clamp your foot to the pedal. That's risky riding and falling could be painful.

Two-wheelers are like **mutual funds**, which are a balanced mix of different investments. A **road bike** is like **stock**. A stock is a part of a company that you can buy. If the company makes money, your stock is worth more. If your company loses money, your stock is worth less. Both are riskier, but the chance to make a profit can be far greater in a shorter amount of time.

Bikes Compared to Types of Investments

BIKE	INVESTMENT	RISK	GROWTH	DBL YOUR MONEY
baby bike	jars at home	0	0%	0
tricycle	bank	very low	2–3%	24–36 yrs.
two-wheeler w/training wheels	bond	low	11.7%	6 yrs.
two-wheeler	growth & income mutual fund	med	12.6%	5$\frac{1}{2}$yrs.
road bike	growth stock	med to high	14.6%	5 yrs.

Average financial return 10 yrs. Period ending 6/1/95. *Irwin Business and Investment Almanac, 1996.*

Would you like to know how long it will take to double your money if you keep it in the bank? Look in the right column. Compare it to the number of years for money invested in a growth stock. It's called the Rule of 72. I'll show you how to find this number when I teach you how to use a calculator in Chapter 9. Which investment doubles your money fastest?

If you want your money to grow faster, you'll move it out of the jars into various types of accounts. To open any of these accounts, you will need your social security number. Let's see if you have one.

MY TO DO LIST

Look up the word risk in the dictionary.

CHAPTER EIGHT

Your Social Security Number

Ask your parents if they have a Social Security card for you. If you already have one, you can skip this chapter. Get out your calculator, and go on to the next chapter.

Social Security numbers are given out by the government. It's your identification number. You'll use it for the rest of your life. No one else has the same number. Right now you need it to open a bank account or invest your money.

Sample Social Security Card

The first thing you will need is an application. You can request one by calling 1-800-772-1213. Ask your parents or guardians to help you with this. You'll reach a recorded set of step-by-step directions. Be prepared to answer five questions; the questions are:

1. your last name (spell it out)
2. your street address (spell it out)
3. your city and state (spell the city)
4. your zip code
5. the number of applications you need (one, two, or three); request one for your brothers or sisters, too

You may also get the form off the Internet. The address is *www.ssa.gov*. After you've dialed in to the site, go to "Forms," then "Application for Social Security card (SS-5)," then download the form with the directions for filling it out.

When you return the application, you'll need to send along proof of your identity, U.S. citizenship, and age. You can use a copy of your birth certificate plus your report card or a copy of your health record from your doctor's office. Ask your parents for help in getting these forms and have them double-check your work.

Several weeks later, you'll receive a social security card with **YOUR SOCIAL SECURITY NUMBER**. Memorize the number. This is an important document. Keep it in a safe place, like in your long-term jar or with your family's important documents. Remember to take it with you to the bank; they need this number to open your account.

MY TO DO LIST

Get a Social Security number.

Memorize my Social Security number.

CHAPTER NINE

Money Math

Q. Is money also math?

A. Yes, it can be added, subtracted, multiplied, and divided.

Calculators make our lives much easier. And they're very funny. They can give you number answers and word answers. Eight numbers also look like letters when you turn the calculator upside down. I'll show you.

Calculator

Take out your calculator. Find the *off* and *on* keys and turn your calculator on. Do you see a 0 in the display window? This is where you see each step of your work and the answer.

A calculator has one key for each number: 1, 2, 3, 4, 5, 6, 7, 8, 9, and 0. It also has keys with the signs for addition, subtraction, multiplication, and division: +, −, ×, and ÷. Then there are these keys: equals, period, and C, which mean equals, decimal point, and clear. Let's have a little fun with number words before we get serious.

$ Press 1 and then press 4. Turn your calculator upside down. What does it say?
$ HI
$ Let's do it again!
$ Press C to clear the display window. Press 1 and 4. Turn your calculator upside down. What does it say?
$ HI
$ And what do you say back? "Hi!"

Calculators are friendly. We'll do another number word later. Let's get down to basics.

ADD

$ Problem: 34 + 56 = 90
$ Press 3 and then 4. Do you see 34 in the window?
$ Press +.
$ Press 5 then 6. Do you see 56 in the window? If you don't, you pressed the wrong keys. Press C to clear and try again.
$ Press =.
$ Does the number 90 show in the display? That's the answer. If some other number shows, go back and try again.
$ Press C or clear until you see a 0 in the display.

SUBTRACT

$ Problem: 98 − 65 = 33
$ Press 9 then 8.
$ Press −.

$ Press 6 then 5.
$ Press =.
$ Do you see 33 in the display? Great!
$ Press C to clear.

MULTIPLY

$ Problem: 638 × 852 = 543,576
$ Press 6 then 3 then 8.
$ Press ×.
$ Press 8 then 5 then 2.
$ Press =.
$ Do you see 543,576?
$ Press C to clear.

DIVIDE

$ Problem: 543,576 ÷ 852 = 638
$ Press 5 then 4 then 3 then 5 then 7 then 6.
$ Press ÷.
$ Press 8 then 5 then 2.
$ Press =.
$ Do you see 638 in the window? Calculators make it much easier to work with big numbers.
$ Press C to clear.

NUMBER WORDS

Now let's try another number word. Upside down 0 is O, 9 is G, 8 is B, 7 is L, 5 is S, 4 is H, 3 is E, and 1 is I. Here's a riddle for you. Do the math problem to find the answer.

Q. One piece of paper money is called a _____. The answer is 2,404 + 5,314.

A. 7,718 or BILL.

Remember to clear your calculator after you do each problem. Press the C key or turn your calculator off, then back on.

THE RULE OF 72

The Rule of 72 is a way to figure out the number of years it will take to double your money, depending on the interest rate. Interest is the money that the bank, for example, gives you when you let them use your money. If the bank says they'll pay you 3 percent interest per year, you will earn 3¢ per dollar each year. Divide 72 by the interest rate you are getting. The result is the number of years it will take for you to double your money.

Let's try 3 percent. How long will it take to double your money if you leave it at the bank earning 3 percent interest?

$ enter 72
$ ÷
$ 3
$ =
$ 24 years to double your money.

Now let's try 10 percent. How long will it take to double your money if it is earning 10 percent?

$ enter 72
$ ÷
$ 10
$ =
$ 7.2 years to double your money.

In this example, one investment will take 24 years to double your money and the other just over 7 years. That's a big difference, isn't it? In Part Three, I'll tell you about different ways to invest your money. I'll let you choose how quickly you want to try to double your money.

MY TO DO LIST

Make my own number—word problem.

PART THREE
Grow It

NOW · SHORT TERM · LONG TERM

CHAPTER TEN

Banks and Tricycles

Here's where the magic begins. If you take the money you've saved to the bank, it will grow while it sits in the bank, whether you add more money or not. It won't grow in the long-term jar at your home, but it will grow in the bank.

Interest Magic

Here's how it grows. When you give the bank your money, the bank lends your money to someone else at a higher rate of interest than the bank pays you. That's how the bank makes money. The bank pays you interest. That's how you make money. If the bank pays 3 percent (3/100) interest, you would make 3 cents (3/100) for every dollar. This is simple interest. But most banks do more. They offer compound interest that pays more than 3 cents at the end of the year. (Compound interest pays interest on top of interest daily instead of once a year.)

Some banks offer special savings programs just for kids through the schools. Some banks will let you have your own account. Others may require your parents to open a custodial account. See what your bank has to offer kids.

You will open similar accounts if you decide to buy bonds, mutual funds, and stocks, so the example below is a good introduction. The type of account isn't as important as opening it and getting started.

Max and Zoë's bank opened accounts for them in their own names and gave them all sorts of goodies: a passbook, an ATM card with a secret code, and interest growing in their account right away. Here's a step-by-step look at opening a bank account.

OPEN AN ACCOUNT

$ Walk in, find the "New Accounts" desk, and tell the bank representative you'd like to open a savings account. He will help you select the best type for your needs.

$ Fill out a new account form. Your parents may want to help you.

MASTER AGREEMENT
PERSONAL DEPOSIT ACCOUNTS

You begin a deposit account relationship with us by giving us information about yourself and by signing below. We enter the information on our computer system.

For most accounts, we give you a Card, which you may use to identify yourself at our branches. You may also use your card for Services if you request a personal identification number (PIN).

The written information we give you is part of this agreement and tells you the current terms of our deposit accounts and Services. We may change these terms at any time. We inform you of changes that affect your rights and obligations.

If more than one person signs below, all accounts are held in joint tenacy with the right of survivorship unless you specify another type of ownership here:

TAXPAYER IDENTIFICATION NUMBER (TIN) TO BE USED FOR DEPOSIT ACCOUNT TAX REPORTING PURPOSES: *Your Soc. Sec. #*
(Check one box only if appropriate)

☐ The signer whose TIN is listed above has been notified by the Internal Revenue Service that he/she is subject to backup withholding because of underreporting of interest or dividends.

☐ No signer is a citizen, resident, or doing business in the United States. Since all signers are considered Non-resident Aliens under United States tax law, each signer is providing his/her permanent foreign address here.

1 *Your address*
2 STREET ADDRESS | CITY, PROVINCE, COUNTRY, POSTAL ZONE
3 STREET ADDRESS | CITY, PROVINCE, COUNTRY, POSTAL ZONE
STREET ADDRESS | CITY, PROVINCE, COUNTRY, POSTAL ZONE

ACCOUNT NAME(S) TYPED:

Your name

We may pay out funds on any <u>one</u> of the signatures below (unless you specify another number here____).

Under penalties of perjury, each signer certifies that the taxpayer information above is correct and complete. Each signer also confirms that all other information given to us is correct.

1 X _____ DATE / /
  SIGNATURE

2 X _____ DATE / /
  SIGNATURE
  SOCIAL SECURITY NO. ☐☐☐ - ☐☐ - ☐☐☐☐

3 X _____ DATE / /
  SIGNATURE
  SOCIAL SECURITY NO. ☐☐☐ - ☐☐ - ☐☐☐☐

Sample New Account Form

$ Take out your Social Security card. You'll enter the number on the new account form.

$ The bank representative will give you an account number that is different from your Social Security number. This number allows the bank to identify your account and find out how much money is in it. You need this number to fill out deposit and withdrawal forms.

DEPOSIT MONEY

Fill out the deposit slip, like the sample deposit slip below. You can find plenty of these forms at the bank counter near the tellers. Use ink; no crayons, pencils, or erasable pens.

$ Write the date and your name and address.
$ For a cash deposit: All bills and coins added together go on the cash line.

Savings Deposit		
	DOLLARS	CENTS
CASH	00	00
CHECKS—LIST SEPARATELY xx-xx/xxxx	00	00
OR TOTAL FROM REVERSE SIDE		
SUBTOTAL	00	00
LESS CASH RECEIVED		
NET DEPOSIT	00	00

ACCOUNT NUMBER

DATE

NAME (PLEASE PRINT)

ADDRESS

CITY   STATE   ZIP CODE

Please sign in teller's presence for cash received.

Savings Deposit

Sample Deposit Slip

$ For a check deposit: If you have a check to deposit, turn it over and "endorse" it as shown in the example below. Write your signature, your account number, and the words "For Deposit Only" above the line. Then enter the check amount in the check line of the deposit form. With each check, be sure to include the fraction in small type located in the upper right; it identifies the bank and branch. Print this number in the check column.

Your name

Your bank name

FOR DEPOSIT ONLY

Your account number

Sample Check Endorsement

$ Then, add the cash and the checks with your calculator (did you remember to bring it?) and enter the total amount in the "subtotal" and "net deposit" lines.

$ Give the completed forms to the person at the "New Accounts" desk. He or she will finish your transaction.

$ Next time you come to the bank with your forms, go directly to the teller. Now comes the good part.

YOUR PASSBOOK

The bank representative may give you back a passbook showing your deposit, the date, your name, and your account number, and the initials of the person at the bank who handled your money. It's your savings history. You will take it with you each time you deposit or withdraw money.

YOUR BANK STATEMENT

If you don't get a passbook, the representative will give you a receipt to save. In addition, you will receive a bank statement in the mail that looks like this. It may come four times a year or monthly.

Statement period:
01/01/99 – 01/31/99
Account Number: xxxxx-xxxxx

❏ **Summary of Your Student Savings Account**

Beginning Balance on 01/01/99	$ 11.40	Annual Percentage Yield earned this period	1.54%
Total Deposits	+ 13.00	Interest paid year-to-date	$ .02
Interest Paid	+ .02		
Ending Balance	$24.42		

❏ **Bank News**

Changing jobs? Retiring? Just call for assistance rolling over funds from your 401(K) or pension plan to an IRA.

❏ **Savings Activity**

Date	Description	Reference Number	Amount
01/25	**Deposits and Credits**		
	Deposit		$ 13.00
	Interest Paid		
01/29	Interest Paid From 04/01/99 Through 06/30/99		$ .02

Sample Monthly Statement

$ Make a file folder with your name on it. Keep your passbook or statement and receipts in the folder. File this folder or give it to your family for their general files. You have just started a credit history. Grownups use a credit history when they want a credit card or a loan. You're getting ready early.

$ Read the statement when it comes.

$ Find the amount of interest the bank is paying you. It may be called Annual Percentage Yield (your total interest).

$ Find your account number. Is it correct?

$ Compare every deposit or withdrawal and the date with your receipts.

$ Find the total amount of interest credited to you.

$ Find your balance, or total, on the date your statement was prepared.

YOUR ATM CARD WITH A SECRET CODE

Some banks don't issue these to kids. Max and Zoë's does. To use your ATM card, you need to pick a PIN (personal identification number). Make it easy. Use your mom's initials or your brother's. Write your PIN down and keep it in your file folder because you have to remember it. It's a secret code. You will have to enter it into a machine several times before you can use it for the first time at the ATM machine outside the bank. Keep your ATM card in a safe place. You can use it to deposit checks and bills but not coins. You have to go inside the bank to deposit coins.

THE ATM MACHINE

$ What power! A plastic card like grown-ups use. Walk up to the ATM machine and follow the directions. Let's call it a mechanical bank teller; open 24 hours a day, seven days a week, and holidays, too. ATMs are everywhere.

$ Put the card in the slot just like the diagram tells you.

$ Read the directions on the display. If you're too short, find an ATM machine for people who use wheelchairs; they will be lower to the ground and may be perfect for your height.

$ Find the deposit envelope for your check or cash. You may have to open a drawer or lift a lever to find them.

$ With this magic plastic card, you can also withdraw cash. There's only one time I suggest withdrawing some of your money and I'll tell you about that later.

$ The machine will spit out a paper receipt. File it and check your monthly statement to make sure it was recorded.

MY TO DO LIST

Open a savings account.

CHAPTER ELEVEN

Big Deal

Stop for a second. Are you feeling proud of yourself? I'll bet. This is a big deal. You've started to take control of an important part of your life. Right now, the kids and I would love to know how you're doing. If you'd like, e-mail us through the web site, *www.kidsfinance.com*. We'd love to hear from you.

But as you head home empowered by your very own savings account, you may say, "Now what do I do?"

The answer is simple. Do it all over again. Keep putting some of your money in your long-term jar. When it fills up or you just feel like going to the bank, deposit it. Watch your money in the bank grow safely and slowly.

A Bigger Deal

Let's say you've saved $100. Now that you have a wad of dough, you might want to find a place where it can grow more quickly. Instead of saving you may decide to invest. An investment is riskier because you could lose it all. You could also make a lot more, if you hold your investment for ten or more years.

I think you're ready to hear a story about investing. It may help you understand risk. I'll use a bike example, just for fun. *This is only an example. It's not investment advice.*

Say your bike is made by a company called Cannondale. You love your bike. You love it so much that you've told your friends they should buy bikes just like yours. When you rode it to school, everybody asked where you bought it. Wow, you say to yourself. I wonder how many Cannondales my bike shop sold this week?

Now something funny seems to be going on. Everywhere you look, you see Cannondale bikes. In front of the library. In front of the grocery store. In a photo of your mom's friend in Colorado. What's going on? Do you just have Cannondale on the brain?

You drop by the bike shop one day. The salesperson is helping other customers. When she's finished, you ask, "Have you sold many Cannondales this week?"

And she replies, "Boy, have we ever! I had to call the company this morning because we're almost sold out. It's a great company."

Then the customer she'd been helping speaks up. "Did you hear? The stock went up to 22 today."

The salesperson says, "I know. I bought it at 14. I've made money so far—pretty exciting, isn't it? Did you know Cannondale sponsors three pro racing teams: road, mountain bike, and wheelchair? And their bikes are winning."

"Yeah, I read that. They're making off-road motorcycles, too. Their products say *Handmade in USA* and are sold worldwide. That's what I like."

What these bike lovers are talking about is investing. They used their money to buy shares of stock in this company. They're part owners of Cannondale. If you buy stock in a company and it does well—sells a lot of bikes, in this case—the company may make a **profit.** It can share that profit with the stockholders. This money is called a **dividend.** Then when the person who bought the stock at $14 a share sells it at $22 a share, she will have made an additional profit of $8 per share. Using her investment or **capital** of $14, she will have made $8 plus a dividend.

If the $14 had stayed in a savings account that paid 3 percent interest, it would have made 42 cents. The question is, if you had $14 to invest, would you rather make $8 or 42 cents? I think the answer is $8.

Who wouldn't? But think again about risk. What if Cannondale started making lousy bikes? What if bike riding stopped being popular and nobody bought bikes? What would have happened then? That share may have been worth less, not more. The investor took a risk and won. But she might have lost, too.

Just as you go to the bike store to buy a bike, you go to the securities market to buy an investment. But because there are so many different kinds of securities, you shop for them not in a store, but in a newspaper or on-line. The newspaper stock pages and the Internet are your securities store. You can pick and choose from a long list of bonds, mutual funds, and stocks. Easy, isn't it? You don't even have to leave your home. But you do have to study the companies you pick before you choose your investment. Ask for help. Most grown-ups are happy to help kids who want to learn how to be responsible about money.

MY TO DO LIST
Pat myself on the back.

CHAPTER TWELVE

Bonds and Two-Wheelers with Training Wheels

Let's take a look at bonds first. A bond is a kind of loan agreement. When you buy a bond, you are lending money to a company for a fixed interest rate and a fixed period of time—for example, 11 percent for one year. In return, the company promises to pay you the interest plus the money you loaned. It sounds a lot like putting your money in the bank. But it's different. Bonds usually pay a higher rate of interest, and the company will use your money only for the amount of time you agreed on—no more, but no less, either. With bank investments, you can take your money out of the bank any time you want.

Bonds may be issued by the U.S. government, state and local governments, and corporations. Bonds get grades that are sort of like the grades you get in school. The highest grade a bond can receive is Aaa and goes from there to Aa, A, Baa, Ba, B, Caa, Ca, C. The higher the grade (Aaa), the less risk you take and the less interest you will earn. The lower the grade (C), the more risk you take and the more interest you could earn for taking that risk.

Corporate Bonds

Let's use a corporate bond as an example. If you buy a ten-year bond for $100, you are loaning the company $100 for ten years. The company agrees to pay you 11 percent interest each year for ten years and will return your $100 at the end of ten years. So the good news is that you get more interest than at a bank. The bad news is you are limited by a fixed rate of interest. You do not participate in the company's profit. That's why bonds are usually less risky than mutual funds and stocks.

Think again about the two-wheeler with training wheels. The extra wheels keep you from tipping over. You might not be able to go very fast, but you will get where you want to go. That's like having a fixed interest rate. You may not make money as quickly as with mutual funds or stocks, but you will make more than in your savings account at the bank.

MY TO DO LIST
Find bond listings in the newspaper.

CHAPTER THIRTEEN

Mutual Funds and Two-Wheelers

When you own a mutual fund, you are buying shares of a company that buys and sells other investments. The interest rate will go up or down depending on how all the investments do together. They're easy to own because a paid professional manages the daily performance of each investment. You don't have the responsibility. First you decide on a company and then you decide which group of investments you like best.

Choosing a mutual fund is like going to the bike store to pick out a two-wheeler. Suddenly, you discover you have many choices. Do you want a bike with road tires, dirt tires, cross tires, pedals with straps, pedals with toe clips, a hard seat or a soft seat? You choose a bike with the features you want.

How do you choose a mutual fund? Since our strategy has been long-term investing, we'll compare two growth funds as an example. This is an example only—*not* a recommendation to buy.

Compare Two Funds

Look in the business section of the Sunday newspaper under mutual funds. They're listed alphabetically. Find Stein Roe funds in bold (the company or fund family). Then find the type of growth investing fund called the Young Investor fund (YngInv). Underline the row of numbers; it's easier to read them this way. Enter Stein Roe and YngInv in the following chart in the Fund #1, Fund Family column.

Let's pick another long-term growth fund to compare it to. Go to Vanguard Index Funds in bold and "500" below. Underline the row of numbers. Enter Vanguard Index and 500 in the Fund #2, Fund Family column. You can use the chart below over and over to compare funds over time. Remember to date your charts. Dates help you compare.

Mutual Fund Chart

FUND 1 DATE	FUND FAMILY FUND NAME	NAV	1-YR % RET.	3-YR %RET.
	Stein Roe YngInv			

FUND 2 DATE	FUND FAMILY FUND NAME	NAV	1-YR % RET.	3-YR %RET.
	Vanguard Index 500			

Now go back to each of the two funds in the newspaper. Do you notice a lowercase letter after the name of your fund? You'll find these letters explained in a box that tells you how to read the tables. The letters tell you about extra charges cutting into your profit: "n" means no-load or no extra charges.

$ Look at the headings across the top of the chart. Find the same headings in your newspaper. Enter the figures.

$ **NAV** means **net asset value**. This is the cost of one share in the whole fund.

$ **1-YR. % Ret**. One-year total return.

$ **3-YR. % Ret**. Three-year total return. Over three years, is the fund performing the same as this year (1-YR % RET.)? Or is it doing better or worse?

Compare the two funds. Is one number larger than the other in the 1-YR % RET. column? Is one number larger in the 3-YR % RET. column? Which is more expensive per share? Are both no-load funds?

Questions to Ask

Now that you know where these funds are listed in the paper, you may begin to hear people talk about them. Some funds may advertise on TV, through magazines, or by mail. Some funds love kids who invest; they have contests and write newsletters. Track those companies just like we did above. When you want more information, call the fund from the telephone number listed in the newspaper chart and ask them to send you their annual report and their prospectus. Go to the library reference desk and ask to look in mutual fund directories. You'll get some answers to four very important questions.

$ Who is running the company behind the family of funds?

$ Who is managing the particular fund? What is the person's background?

$ How well is the fund performing compared to other funds of its kind?

$ Do investors pay for the manager's services?

When you own several investments, you may want one or more to be a mutual fund. It would leave some of your saved money growing with a paid professional watching over it.

Next we'll move on to stocks, the road bikes of the investment world. Fasten your bike helmet. Coming up are some delicate tips to master to give you a truly great ride.

MY TO DO LIST
Pick a mutual fund
to research.

CHAPTER FOURTEEN

Stocks and Road Bikes

Think big. Would you like to own a company like Nike, Sony, or IBM? You might one day. But in the meantime, you can buy stock. When you own stock, you become a part owner of that company and its profits. As a stockholder, you may be able to make money two different ways.

A Double Whammy

1. First, if the company grows and earns money, it may pay you, as part owner, cash from this profit. This payment is called a **dividend**.
2. Then, if lots of people want to buy what the company sells, the stock price may go up. If you buy stock and hold it for a while—say ten years—the stock price may go up and it may go down, but over time, it usually goes up. Then you can sell it for more than you paid for it.

When you look at the stock market pages in the newspaper, though, you see a zillion stocks to choose from. How do you decide which one you want to buy? Do some homework. You want to buy stock in companies that are going to stay in business and do well. Which ones are those? Think about this list of questions to help you decide.

Stockpicking—
Eeny, meeny,
miny, moe

$ What do I buy? I buy what I like.

$ What do I like?

$ Do other people buy what I like?

$ Is the product popular only in the United States or do people buy it all over the world?

$ Is there more than one brand? Do they all cost about the same?

$ Is one brand better than the others?

$ Is the company's management honest and skilled, and do they seem to be looking ahead?

Take your time. Go slowly. This is your road bike, and it's a bit riskier because the tires are skinny and there are lots of gears. There's no professional doing the work for you as with the mutual fund. You're on your own. I've made you a sample "What do I like?" chart and filled it in. Think about my answers and then fill in your answers.

What Do I Like

QUESTION: What do I like	1ST CHOICE	2ND CHOICE	3RD CHOICE	4TH CHOICE	5TH CHOICE	6TH CHOICE
to eat	McDonalds	Hershey kisses	Cheerios	chips		
to drink	Coke	Sprite	oj	choc milk		
to wear	Oakleys	tevas	big dog	Nikes		
to read	R.L. Stine	SPILL for kids	Nickelodeon	Boxcar Children	Nancy Drew	
to own	CD player	computer	collectible baseball card	Dodgers jacket	front/row Laker seats	bicycle

What Do I Like

QUESTION: What do I like	1ST CHOICE	2ND CHOICE	3RD CHOICE	4TH CHOICE	5TH CHOICE	6TH CHOICE
to eat						
to drink						
to wear						
to read						
to own						

Good job! Once you have identified what you like, you can start looking for companies that own the products or services. So, using my chart as an example, you could look at companies like McDonalds, Nike, General Mills (which makes Cheerios), Sony, and Topps (which prints baseball cards).

If you buy stock in a company whose product you like, you'll look forward to checking the stock pages. So let's get out the newspaper and go shopping. Find the business section and turn to the back pages. We'll start with our bike made by Cannondale.

The Stock Supermarket

The stock market pages are full of columns with numbers and symbols. They look confusing. But once you know how to read them, like the mutual fund tables, you'll see that each line tells a story. The print is very tiny, so you may want to use a magnifying glass.

To find our company, you'll need to look in three stock exchanges. All three list the companies in alphabetical order. They are the New York Stock Exchange (NYSE), the National Association of Securities Dealers Automated Quotation, usually referred to as NASDAQ, and the American Stock Exchange (AMEX), which is owned by NASD. The exchanges must follow rules established by the Securities and Exchange Commission (SEC), a federal agency. These rules protect you and your investment, but cannot guarantee your profit.

You'll find Cannondale in the NASDAQ section. Look under the Cs. In the newspaper, Cannondale may be shortened to Canondle. Draw a line under the whole row so that you're sure you're reading the right line.

A Stock Story

The chart below shows what was going on with Cannondale on December 4, 1998. On the blank row below, you can fill in the numbers you've just underlined in the newspaper. Here's what the column headings mean:

Stock Report

52-week high	52-week low	Stock	Div	Yield %	P/E Ratio	Sales 100s	High	Low	Last	Chg
$28^1/_4$	$7^5/_8$	Canondle	...	...	8	992	$10^3/_{16}$	$8^{15}/_{16}$	$8^{15}/_{16}$	$-^{15}/_{16}$

$ **52-week high and low:** The numbers tell us the highest and lowest price paid for a share of Cannondale during the past 52 weeks, or one year. The numbers are expressed as fractions of a dollar so that $28^1/_4$ translates to $28.25. The numbers have always been reported as fractions of a dollar. However, after April 2001 all U.S. stocks will be reported as decimals. If you know the highs and lows over a year, you can compare them to the stock's price today. A company whose 52-week high is pretty close to its 52-week low is a less risky investment than a company whose highs and lows are far apart. You can also compare Cannondale's figures to those of other companies by looking up and down the news-paper columns.

The following chart shows the fractions as cents.

Fraction Equivalents

FRACTION	DOLLARS	CENTS
$1/16$	$ .06	6¢
$1/8$	$ .125	12.5¢
$1/4$	$ .25	25¢
$3/8$	$ .375	37.5¢
$1/2$	$ .50	50¢
$5/8$	$ .675	67.5¢
$3/4$	$ .75	75¢
$7/8$	$ .875	87.5¢
1	$1.00	100¢

$ **Stock:** Each stock has a ticker symbol. BIKE is Cannondale's symbol on NASDAQ. Stockbrokers use this symbol to identify a stock.

$ **Div:** Dividend. The dollar amount of the company's annual profits per share that Cannondale would pay stockholders. But Cannondale isn't paying a dividend. They're putting their profit back into the business.

$ **Yield %:** Rate of return. How big or small the dividend is compared to the price of one share of stock. Divide the dividend by the current price of the stock. If you want high income from your stock, look for a high yield. Look up and down that column in the newspaper to compare company yields.

$ **P/E Ratio:** Price/earnings ratio. This is the last price of the day for a share of stock (LAST, here $8^{15}/_{16}$ or $8.94) divided by the company's profit or earnings per share (EPS) for the last year. To figure out the earnings per share, divide the LAST (8.94) by the P/E ratio (8). Cannondale earned about $1.12 per share last year. Understanding this ratio will help you decide if a stock is over- or underpriced. You would be paying 8 times Cannondale's yearly earnings per share to purchase one share of its company.

$ **Sales 100s:** The number of shares traded during the day divided by 100. 99,200 shares of Cannondale's stock were bought and sold on the business day before the date on the newspaper (Friday, December 4, 1998). Friday's numbers are the story from Thursday's trading.

   Compare this figure over a period of time with sales figures for other stocks to find out if Cannondale is an active or inactive stock. Check for sudden increases or decreases in the number of shares traded. These changes could mean good news or bad news.

   $ Perhaps people are buying this stock because the company has just announced it will sell a new, lighter, faster, and cheaper bike than the other bike companies.

   $ Maybe the quarterly report showed a drop in profits, and so stockholders decided to sell their shares.

$ **High and Low:** The high and low for *one day*. The first two numbers tell us the high and the low for *one year*. On our chart the highest price paid during the day was $10.19 ($10^{3}/_{16}$) and the lowest price paid was $8.94 ($8^{15}/_{16}$).

$ **Last:** The last price paid at the end of the day [$8.94 or $(8^{15}/_{16})$]. If you look at the high, low, and last figures, you'll see the range of Cannondale's selling prices for the day. During trading hours, the stock rose as high as $10^{3}/_{16}$, dropped as low as $8^{15}/_{16}$, and closed at $8^{15}/_{16}$.

$ **Chg:** The difference between the last price of the day ($8^{15}/_{16}$) and the last price of the day the previous day ($9^{7}/_{8}$). The difference was $^{15}/_{16}$ of a dollar less than the day before. You read $-^{15}/_{16}$ as down fifteen-sixteenths.

Pick Them and Track Them

Now that I've explained my row of numbers, compare your figures from the newspaper to mine in the chart. Are they higher? Lower? About the same? Is the company paying a dividend? Does it look to you as if Cannondale has done well?

Now that you know how to read the stock pages, pick a few stocks and track them for several weeks. Are the prices going up or down? If other investors are buying the stock and prices go up, this is known as a bull market. If they are selling and driving the price down, this is known as a bear market. If the stock stays at least the same each day or goes up, you may decide to buy it. If it goes way down, it may also be a great buy.

Here are some charts to use to track your stocks: name of the stock, the yearly high and low, the daily high and low, the yield, and the P/E ratio. Compare the stocks to themselves and to each other over a few weeks or months and see how they're doing.

Investments I Am Tracking

STOCK 1

	52-week high	52-week low	Div	Yield %	P/E Ratio	Sales 100s	High	Low	Last	Chg
Week 1										
Week 2										
Week 3										

STOCK 2

	52-week high	52-week low	Div	Yield %	P/E Ratio	Sales 100s	High	Low	Last	Chg
Week 1										
Week 2										
Week 3										

STOCK 3

	52-week high	52-week low	Div	Yield %	P/E Ratio	Sales 100s	High	Low	Last	Chg
Week 1										
Week 2										
Week 3										

Compare Them

Now compare the stocks you've followed. Fill in the blanks in the chart below and answer the questions that follow.

Stock Comparisons

STOCK NAME

	52-week high	52-week low	Div	Yield %	P/E Ratio	Sales 100s	High	Low	Last	Chg
Stock 1										
Stock 2										
Stock 3										

1. Which stock is paying the highest dividend?
2. Which stock is the most expensive?
3. Which has the lowest P/E ratio?
4. Which stock traded the most shares?
5. Which stock paid the highest dividend?

Using this information, you may decide whether to buy one of these three stocks or keep looking.

MY TO DO LIST

Fill out the "what do I like" chart.

CHAPTER FIFTEEN

Buy It, Hold It, and Track It

Buy It

Let's say you're ready to buy a stock. What next? You can buy stock several ways. One way is through a stockbroker. A stockbroker is an expert in buying and selling stocks. Someone in your household may already work with a stockbroker. Ask around—maybe one of your classmates' parents is a broker. If you work with stockbrokers, you'll pay a fee for the service they provide.

Or some stockowners work through discount brokers on the Internet to buy and sell shares. You'll pay a fee with an on-line account, too. Ask your parents or guardian to help you open an account. They will have to sign your brokerage accounts until you reach the age of majority.

Let's use a broker and Cannondale as our examples. Your parents can help you place an order.

- $ Call your stockbroker on the phone.
- $ Tell him you want to place an order for ten shares of Cannondale.
- $ He'll say, "Do you know the symbol?" He will look it up on his computer. In a few seconds he reports, "The stock is $13^3/_4$ to $14^1/_4$." This means that $13.75 is the highest price any buyer wants to pay (bid) and $14.25 is the lowest price any seller will take (ask) at the time the quote was given.
- $ Tell him you are willing to pay $14 for the stock.
- $ He may remind you of his transaction fees.
- $ He will send your order to the stock exchange.
- $ You've become an official stockholder in Cannondale.
- $ File away the confirmation statements that the brokerage house will send you. Keep them with your bank files.

Hold It

It may have taken you a few years to go from your baby bike to a two-wheeler. But you ride well now and you have confidence. You might even be able to teach someone else how to ride.

Similarly, over time, stock prices have always gone up or done better. By owning stock when you're young, you can take advantage of how money grows over time. When you are older, you have less time to watch money grow.

When you make investments over time, you take pride in watching them grow. Soon you may have an idea of your own that needs funding to become a business. Or other companies may need your investment to grow. When you are old enough to receive a grown-up paycheck, you will have an additional way to make and invest money.

Be a kid and be a smart kid. Start now saving and investing for life. When you grow up, you'll have the comfort and safety of knowing you can take care of yourself and others. Save a little as often as you can forever.

Track It

Want to have some fun with your new purchase? Let's draw a picture of your stock. Add a dot to this picture every few months with each stock you own. Track it. The whole point of buying smart is to hang onto your stocks for ten or more years. It's after some time has passed that you may see your profits. **BUY and HOLD**; that's the strategy.

First, take a piece of graph paper. On the first line, write the date, the name of your stock, and how many shares you bought. Cut out the stock line from the paper and glue it just under the name, so you'll remember what the stock looked like the day you bought it. (See page 121 for a stock picture.)

$ Count down ten squares from the top and use a ruler to draw a horizontal line across the page. This is your dateline.

$ Count five squares from the left and use a ruler to draw a vertical line the length of the page. This is your dollar line. Looks good so far, doesn't it?

$ Draw a dot where the two lines meet.

$ Count down five lines and make another dot.

$ Continue this to the bottom of the page. Each line represents $1. Each dot represents dollars in multiples of five.

$ Find the middle dot on the dollar line.

$ Pick the number in the fives table that is closest to what you paid for your stock. In our example, you, like the salesperson in the bike store, paid $14 for Cannondale. Fifteen is the closest five multiple, so write 15 in the second row to the left of the middle dot.

$ Then fill in the numbers that are multiples of five above and below fifteen: 20, 25, and then down: 10, 5, 0.

Connect the Dots

You are now ready to enter your first dot. This dot will tell you what you paid for your stock. In this case, it was $14.

$ Go to the dot next to fifteen and count down one square. Each square equals one dollar. Make a dot.

$ Now, write the date of your dot in the first column underneath your horizontal line.

The next time you look in the paper,

$ Write that date under the next vertical line.

$ Find the last trade amount from the paper, say it's 16.

$ Make a dot on the line above the date that stands for 16.

$ Connect the dots at last.

Your stock is beginning to have a shape! So far you've made money. What will your stock's picture look like next week? And the week after? Remember, you bought the stock hoping to keep it for a very, very long time—for the **LONG TERM**. This is our game plan: **BUY AND HOLD**.

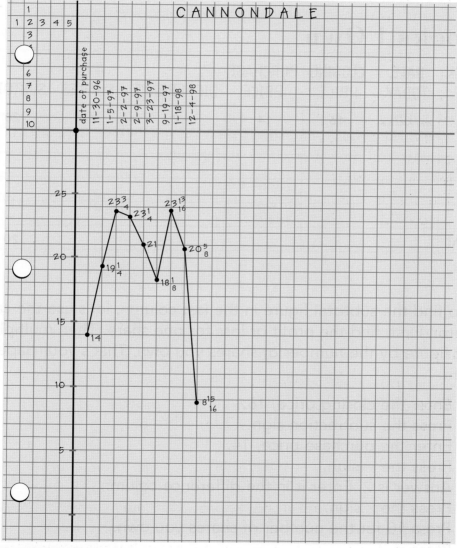

My Stock's Picture

Paper Profits

Fill in the next chart to see how much money you've made or lost on paper according to the price of each stock. Then add the subtotal column to get the profit or loss for all your stocks combined.

Stocks I Own

STOCK NAME	DATE TODAY	CLOSING PRICE	PURCHASE PRICE	DIFFERENCE	# OF SHARES	SUBTOTAL
BIKE	xx/xx/xx	16	14	2	10	20
TOTAL						20

To find the subtotal figure in the last column, let's use the calculator. First, find the profit or loss for one share. Then multiply that figure by the number of shares you own. That's your paper profit.

$ Enter the closing price, 16.
$ Press the subtraction sign −.
$ Enter the purchase price, 14.
$ Press the = sign.
$ Answer is 2. Enter it in the difference column.
$ Press the × sign.
$ Press 10 for the number of shares you own.
$ Press =.

$ Answer $20.

$ In this example, you made $20 on this stock.

If you recall, with stocks you can make money two ways. One, from the profit or loss of the price of the stock. Second, from the dividend paid from the company's profits. If Cannondale paid a dividend, you would multiply the dividend by the number of shares you own. Then add the total dividend to the profit or loss to calculate your *total return*.

MY TO DO LIST
Start a stock graph.

CHAPTER SIXTEEN

Company Stories

Three Winners

Smart investors know the story of each company whose shares they want to buy. With a buy and hold strategy, you might own stock for ten years or more. After ten years a stock will tell a pretty interesting tale.

Let's get smart. We'll look at annual reports, ten-year graphs of a company's stock prices, and charts to see what kind of dividends a company pays over the same time period. We'll piece together the tales of three companies, IBM, Coca-Cola, and Disney.

$ For IBM and Coca-Cola, we'll use information from the companies' annual reports for an inside view and some general information. Call the company you're interested in. They'll be eager to send you the annual report.

$ For all three companies, we'll see how the stock did over ten years by looking at a graph on their price histories. Graphs are easy to find on the Internet. One web site is *http://quote.yahoo.com*. Enter the stock name, click enter, and print the ten-year graph.

$ Then, for all three companies, we'll add up the dividends paid per share for ten years. This information is available at libraries from a public company financial digest called *Value Line*.

At this point, you will be able to compare the total return of the three companies. These examples may help you compare stocks you're thinking of buying in the future.

IBM

Let's start with IBM by looking at the annual report. The annual report can be fun to read because in the opening letter, the chairman of the board gives you an insider's point of view. After that, you'll find pages of numbers that tell you about money coming into the company, money going out, and money that became profit from the previous year.

So, let's see what Lou Gerstner, the head of IBM, had to say in 1995. First, he writes, IBM is the world's largest information technology services company. It is also the world's largest software company. IBM was even the leading computer company in China. The company had 80,000 employees who were rewarded for doing excellent work.

Then he went on to say that in 1993 the company was *losing* $8 billion. In 1995, though, they were making $4.2 billion. Wow! What a change! Mr. Gerstner must have put in a lot of hard work, but he gives a lot of credit to his employees, too. In the closing paragraphs of the annual report, he thanks his employees. "You never, never, never quit," he writes. "Others said IBM was dead, but you rolled up your sleeves, picked up the bricks and rebuilt your company, day by day, product by product, customer by customer. Whenever I was in the IBM world, at night I saw the lights still on in your offices. The next morning, I saw all the empty pizza boxes . . . I'm very proud to work alongside you. Thank you."

Companies employ people just like your parents and their friends. These people who work in a company are important, but we can't forget the numbers. Let's look at IBM's price history over about ten years.

IBM STOCK PRICE GRAPH 1985–1995

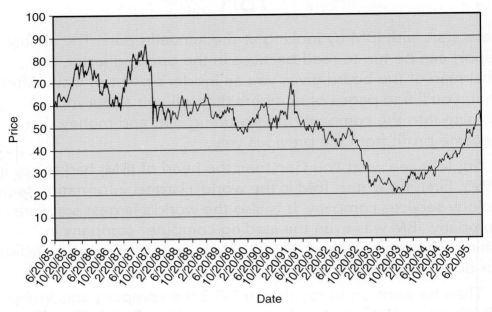

10+-Year Stock Price Graph

$ In June 1985, each share of the stock traded at $61.

$ In June 1989, three years later, the stock dropped $5 a share and traded at $56.

$ In June 1992, after another three years, the price dropped to $46.

$ In September 1993, it sank to $21.

$ In August 1995, it rose to $56 again.

$ In 1998, it shot up to $137 per share!

So you can see that the price of one share of IBM had a lot of ups and downs over ten years. If you'd bought stock in 1985 and sold it ten years later, you would have lost $5 per share—the price dropped from $61 per share to $56 per share. It was a very flat graph. And if you had held onto your stock just a few more years, you would have made $76 per share!

What about dividends? Remember, Cannondale was not paying dividends. Instead, the company put profits back into the company. IBM, though, did pay dividends—$20.22 per share over that ten-year period.

Coca-Cola

Coca-Cola stock figures tell a very different story. If you'd owned stock in that company for about ten years, you would have made seven times your money, for a profit of $21 per share. The company paid a $2.16 per share dividend over that period, too. Here's the graph showing what happened to Coke stock.

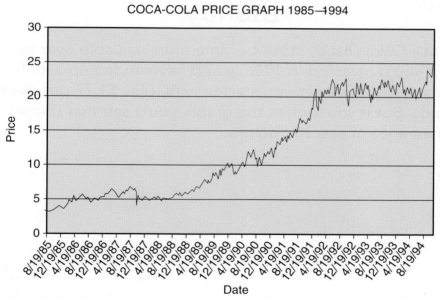

COCA-COLA PRICE GRAPH 1985–1994

10+-Year Stock Price Graph

$ In August 1985, the stock traded at $3 per share.

$ In January 1988, the stock traded at $5 per share.

$ In April 1990, the stock traded at $10 per share.

$ In June 1992, the stock traded at $20 per share.

$ In September 1994, the stock traded at $24 per share.

What happened? The numbers in the annual report tell that story: basically, Coke simply became very popular. More people in Great Britain drink Coca-Cola than drink tea. More people in France drink Coca-Cola than drink bottled mineral water, a traditional French favorite. Coca-Cola even outsells the leading coffee manufacturer in Brazil.

Disney

Like Coca-Cola, Disney stock became more valuable over ten years. If you'd invested in 1986, you'd have ended up with five times as much money as you started with, plus $1.77 per share in dividends. But if you look at the graph, you'll see that Disney stock had a lot of ups and downs.

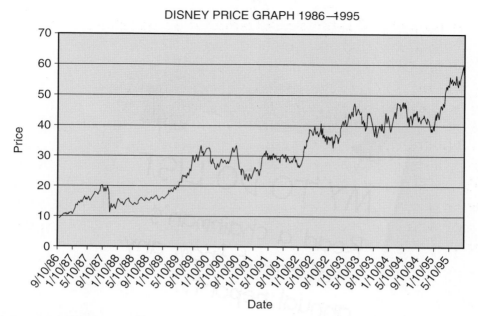

DISNEY PRICE GRAPH 1986—1995

10+-Year Stock Price Graph

$ In September 1986, the stock traded at $10 per share.

$ In September 1987, the stock traded at $19 per share.

$ In July 1990, the stock rose again to $29 per share.

$ In April 1992, the stock traded at $38 per share.

$ In November 1994, the stock traded at $43 per share.

$ In June 1995, the stock traded at $58 per share.

I suggest that you make graphs of all the stocks you own or might like to own. This helps you to remember accurately what happened over time.

MY TO DO LIST

Read a chairman's statement from any annual report.

CHAPTER SEVENTEEN

Do It

If you've taken the big plunge by actually buying a stock, mutual fund, or bond, you are now in another world. You are in the galaxy called the financial universe. While you are here on earth, your money is out there making magic. If you make the right choices, your money could grow enough in ten or twenty years to allow you to explore life without limit. To explore life beyond the lid.

We end this book where we began: picking out a special coin or bill to put in your LONG-TERM jar. But now you know where to look for your own money, how to ask for money, and what you might do to earn it. You know that you must save some of what you find, get, and earn. Once you've saved it, you now know how to grow it.

What's left?

DO IT!

Start by selecting the first coin or bill that will get you started. Decorate it. You'll want to remember which coin or bill changed the way you live your life. Now, put it in the LONG-TERM jar and close the lid.

The rest is up to you. I believe in you and your ability to find lucky pennies and even nifty fifties. I believe in your ability to save, invest, and keep track of your money. And when you do, if you want to tell a friend, tell Max, Zoë, and me. We'll be happy to hear from you. Write to us *at www.kidsfinance.com.*

My best to you,

Hollis

Hollis—Max and Zoë's mom

MY TO DO LIST

Make sure the lid of
my LONG-TERM jar
is on real tight.
Check out the web site
www.kidsfinance.com.

PART FOUR

Fun with It

NOW SHORT TERM LONG TERM

CHAPTER EIGHTEEN

Money Games

Word Search

```
C   A   L   C   U   L   A   T   O   R   T
S   M   L   Y   E   D   N   R   M   C   A
B   I   L   L   H   A   P   I   J   O   C
K   L   S   Y   O   K   Y   S   H   I   K
J   C   X   J   L   W   M   K   L   N   B
T   M   D   O   L   L   A   R   J   L   P
S   N   I   B   I   N   G   N   I   A   E
X   H   M   L   S   K   I   V   C   D   R
U   P   E   N   N   Y   C   D   S   E   T
```

Find these words and circle them.

allowance	job	dollar
coin	bill	risk
calculator	magic	dime
Hollis	penny	jar

Crossword Puzzle

DOWN

1. where you find stock quotes
2. place where your money makes 3%
5. shares of —— (name the word)

ACROSS

3. name the machine at the bank where you use a credit card to get money out
4. bank records your deposits here
5. in a bank your money is —— (4 letters; how risky)
6. the name of money you make expressed as a percent

See p. 151 for answers.

Multiple Choice

1. A stock exchange resembles _____.

   (a) a bike store.

   (b) a bank.

   (c) your bedroom.

2. Stocks are listed in _____.

   (a) the *Lands End* catalogue.

   (b) the phone book.

   (c) the newspaper business section.

3. The American Stock Exchange (AMEX) is _____.

   (a) an annual stock report.

   (b) a stock table.

   (c) a kind of bike.

4. The financial pages of a newspaper tell us information about _____.

   (a) bikes for sale.

   (b) your horoscope.

   (c) publicly traded companies.

Matching

MATCH COLUMN A WITH COLUMN B

match each column by drawing a line

COLUMN A

road bike

baby bike

two-wheeler

two-wheeler w/training wheels

COLUMN B

mutual fund

bond

bank

stock

COLUMN A

now jar

short-term jar

long-term jar

COLUMN B

go to the bank

spend

spend or save

COLUMN A

KO

DIS

BIKE

IBM

P/E ratio

dividends

broker

COLUMN B

Disney

Coca-Cola

International Business Machines

Cannondale

Amount of profit a company pays its stockholders

Shows whether investors are willing to pay a lot or a little for a stock

Person licensed to sell stocks, mutual funds, etc.

MATCH THE DENOMINATIONS

$1	Lincoln
$2	Washington
$5	Franklin
$10	Jefferson
$20	Grant
$50	Hamilton
$100	Jackson

COIN GAMES

ADD YOUR PILES

Separate your coins into piles

$ COUNT THE NICKELS   5, 10, 15 . . . (5 times table).
$ COUNT THE DIMES   10, 20, 30 . . . (10 times table).
$ Add each pile separately. Write down each amount.
$ Add all the piles together for the TOTAL. (Use your calculator for practice if you want to.)

MAKE A COIN BUCK

Place a $1 bill in front of you. Then start coin piles. Each must add up to 100 cents. Look how high the penny pile is compared to the quarter pile. Those piles equal one flat dollar bill! Feel the difference in their weight.

FLIP 'EM

"Heads you win; tails I lose." You can learn to flip or toss coins. Spin them or roll them if flipping is too hard. This is good to know; it can solve many arguments you may have with your sister or brother or mom or dad!

RUB 'EM

You can make coin rubbings. Take aluminum foil and cover your coin. Then take the flat side of a pencil and rub it over the top. Now lift off the foil. See the design? Lay a piece of paper over any coin. Rub your crayon over it. Check it out!

COIN-PRESSIONS

Now take modeling clay. Press any coin into it. Gently take it out. See the impression?

CHAPTER NINETEEN

Money Words

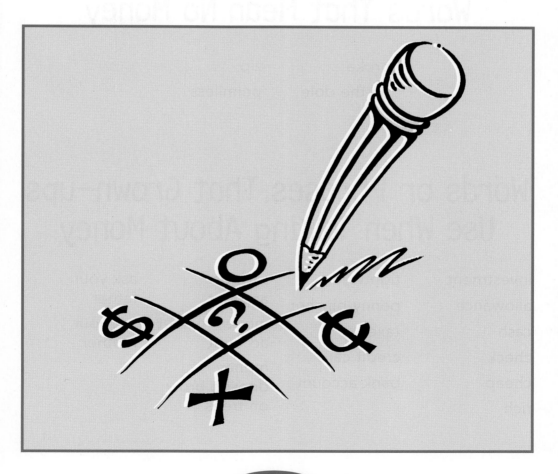

Words That Mean Money

small change	dough	funny money	rainy day fund
big money	bread	one G	payoff
nifty fifty	wad	a buck	score
loose change	pile	pin money	loot
spare change	lump sum	a clam	haul
purse strings	found money	nest egg	

Words That Mean No Money

broke	zip
on the dole	penniless

Words or Phrases That Grown-ups Use When Talking About Money

investment	tightwad	savings account	ask your father
allowance	penny-pincher		
cash	taxes	money market account	ask your mother
check	credit card		
cheap	bank account	money doesn't grow on trees	
rich			

Quotes to Think About

A penny saved is a penny earned.

—Benjamin Franklin (reportedly)

We can do no great thing; only small things, with great love.

—Mother Teresa

The will to win is not nearly as important as the will to prepare to win.

—Anonymous

To accomplish great things, we must not only act, but also dream; not only plan, but also believe.

—Anatole France

It's not what you make; it's what you keep.

—Famous financial phrase

Killing time murders opportunities.

—Anonymous

Education's purpose is to replace an empty mind with an open one.

—Malcolm S. Forbes

The future belongs to those who believe in the beauty of their dreams.

—Eleanor Roosevelt

Opportunity is missed by most people because it is dressed in overalls and looks like work.

—Thomas A. Edison

Happiness resides in activity.

—Aristotle

The hero is no braver than an ordinary man, but he is brave five minutes longer.

—Ralph Waldo Emerson

Solutions to Money Games

CROSSWORD PUZZLE

Down

1. newspaper
2. bank
5. stock

Across

3. ATM
4. passbook
5. safe
6. interest

MULTIPLE CHOICE

1. (a)
2. (c)
3. (b)
4. (c)

MATCHING

road bike → stock
baby bike → bank
two-wheeler → mutual fund
two-wheeler w/training wheels → bond
now jar → spend
short-term jar → spend or save
long-term jar → go to the bank

KO → Coca-Cola
DIS → Disney
Bike → Cannondale
IBM → International Business Machines
P/E → shows whether investors are willing to pay a lot or a little for a stock
dividends → amount of profit a company pays its stockholders
broker → person licensed to sell stocks, mutual funds, etc.

MATCH THE DENOMINATIONS

$1 → Washington
$2 → Jefferson
$5 → Lincoln
$10 → Hamilton
$20 → Jackson
$50 → Grant
$100 → Franklin

Appendices

Allowance Job Chart

TO DO	S	M	T	W	TH	F	SA
Recycling							
Newspapers							
Trash							
Set table							
Clear table							

TO DO	S	M	T	W	TH	F	SA
Recycling							
Newspapers							
Trash							
Set table							
Clear table							

TO DO	S	M	T	W	TH	F	SA
Recycling							
Newspapers							
Trash							
Set table							
Clear table							

Write your initial in the box under the day of the week and next to the job you did.

Glossary of Terms

Bank seal	Seal on bill that shows the federal district where the bill comes from.
Bonds	A loan you make to a company in return for interest.
Bureau of Engraving and Printing	Part of the Treasury Department that makes bills.
Capital	Money you invest.
Compound interest	Interest paid on capital and interest calculated daily.
Counterfeit	Imitation or fake.
Credit history	Record of how you spend your money and pay your debts.
Dividend	Sum of money paid to investors out of company profits.
Federal Reserve System	National banking system in charge of money supply in the United States.
Great Seal	Seal on bills that symbolizes different parts of the U.S. government.
Interest	Money paid when you loan your money for use by a bank or company.
Mint	Part of the Treasury Department that manufactures coins.
Mint mark	Letter on some coins that shows at which mint they were made.

Mutual funds	Pools of money used to buy stocks, bonds, and other securities for a group of investors.
Profit	Money that's left after a person or company has paid its bills and expenses.
Risk	The possibility that you'll lose money when investing.
Secretary of the Treasury	Head of the Treasury Department.
Securities	General term referring to stocks and bonds.
Serial number	Series of one prefix letter, eight numbers, and one suffix letter on each bill. Newer bills have two prefix letters.
Share	The unit of a company that you buy as an investment.
Simple interest	Interest paid on capital only.
Stockbroker	An expert in buying and selling securities.
Stockholders	People who own shares in a company.
Stocks	Shares of a company that you may buy.
Treasurer of the United States	Assistant to the Secretary of the Treasury.
Treasury Department	Federal government department in charge of money in the United States.

Index of Figures, Tables, and Graphs

FIGURES

TABLES AND GRAPHS

Additional Resources

BOOKS

Adler, David A. *Banks: Where the Money Is.* New York: Franklin Watts, 1985.

Adler, David A. *Calculator Fun.* New York: Franklin Watts, 1981.

Anderson, Shane M. *The Complete Lincoln Cent Encyclopedia.* Iola: Krause Publications, 1996.

Berg, Adriane, and Arthur Berg Bochner. *The Totally Awesome Money Book.* New York: Newmarket Press, 1993.

Berger, Melvin and Gilda. *Round and Round the Money Goes.* Nashville: Ideals Children's Books, 1993.

Berry, Joy. *Every Kid's Guide to Making and Managing Money.* Chicago: Children's Press, 1987.

Buehr, Walter. *TREASURE: The Story of Money and Its Safeguarding.* New York: G.P. Putnam's Sons, 1955.

Dunnan, Nancy. *Banking.* Parsippany: Silver Burdett, 1990.

Floherty, John J. *Money-Go-Round.* Philadelphia and New York: J. B. Lippincott, 1964.

Fodor, R. V. *Nickels, Dimes, and Dollars.* New York: William Morrow, 1980.

Friedlander, Joanne K., and Jean Neal. *Stock Market abc.* Chicago: Follett, 1969.

Godfrey, Neale S. *A Penny Saved.* New York: Simon & Schuster, 1995.

Kent, Zachary. *The Story of The New York Stock Exchange.* Chicago: Children's Press, 1990.

Little, Jeffrey B. *Wall Street—How It Works.* New York: Chelsea House, 1988.

Maestro, Betsy. *The Story of Money.* New York: Clarion Books, 1993.

Morgan, Tom. *Money, Money, Money: How to Get and Keep It.* New York: G. P. Putnam's Sons, 1978.

Neal, Harry Howard. *Money.* New York: Julian Messner, 1967.

Otfinoski, Steve. *The Kid's Guide to Money: Earning It, Saving It, Spending It, Growing It, Sharing It.* New York: Scholastic, 1996.

Parker, Nancy Winslow. *Money, Money, Money.* New York: HarperCollins, 1995.

Seuling, Barbara. *You Can't Count a Billion Dollars & Other Little Known Facts About Money.* Garden City: Doubleday, 1979.

Sobol, Rose and Donald. *Stocks and Bonds.* New York: Franklin Watts, 1963.

Spies, Karen Bornemann. *Our Money.* Brookfield: The Millbrook Press, 1992.

Sterling, Dorothy. *Wall Street: The Story of the Stock Exchange.* Garden City: Doubleday, 1955.

Wallace, G. David. *Money Basics.* Englewood Cliffs: Prentice-Hall, Inc., 1984.

Wilkinson, Elizabeth. *Making Cents; Every Kid's Guide to Money.* Boston: Little, Brown and Company, 1989.

Weinstein, Grace W. *Money of Your Own.* New York: E. P. Dutton, 1977.

Wetterau, Bruce. *Congressional Quarterly's Desk Reference on American Government.* Washington: Congressional Quarterly, Inc., 1995.

Television

CNBC Nightly Business Report. PBS
Wall Street Week with Louis Rukeyser. PBS

BROKERS' WEB SITES

Charles Schwab: www.schwab.com
E*Trade: www.etrade.com
National Discount Brokers: www.ndb.com
Quick & Reilly: www.quick-reilly.com

OTHER WEB SITES

American Stock Exchange: www.amex.com
Barron's Online: www.barrons.com
CNBC: www.cnbc.com
CNBC Student Stock Tournament: http://sst.cnbc.com
Girls, Inc.: www.girlsinc.org
Go Kids: www.go.com/center/kids
Hollywood Stock Exchange: www.hsx.com
JumpStart!: Financial Smarts for Students:
    www.jumpstartcoalition.org
Junior Achievement: www.ja.org
Library of Congress: www.loc.gov
NASDAQ: www.nasdaq.com
New York Stock Exchange: www.nyse.com
Save for America: www.schoolsavings.com
SaveLab: www.plan.ml.com/family/kids

Stock Market Game: *www.smg2000.org*

Tomorrow's Morning: *www.morning.com*

The Wall Street Journal Interactive Edition: *www.wsj.com*

White House for Kids:
   www.whitehouse.gov/WH/kids/html/kidshome.html

Yahoo Quotes: *quote.yahoo.com*

Yahooligans: *www.yahooligans.com*

Young Investor Fund: *www.steinroe.com*

ORGANIZATIONS AND FEDERAL AGENCIES

American Numismatic Association

818 N. Cascade Avenue

Colorado Springs, CO 80903-3279

719-632-2646

American Promise—The Alliance for Youth

909 North Washington Street, Suite 400

Alexandria, VA 22314-1556

888-55-YOUTH

www.americaspromise.org

Biz Tech

National Foundation of Teaching Entrepreneurship (NFTE)

120 Wall Street, 29th Floor

New York, NY 10005

212-232-3333

Board of Governors

Federal Reserve Board
20th and C Streets, NW
Washington, DC 20551
202-452-3204
www.federalreserve.gov/bios

Bureau of Engraving and Printing

Department of the Treasury
14th and C Streets, SW
Washington, DC 20228
202-874-3188
www.bep.treas.gov

Camp Entrepreneur

National Education Center for Women in Business
Seton Hill College/NECWB
Seton Hill Drive
Greensburg, PA 15601
800-632-9248
www.necwb.setonhill.edu

Camp Start-Up

Independent Means
126 Powers Street
Santa Barbara, CA 93103
805-350-1816
www.independentmeans.com

Kiddie Tax

IRS 800-424-FORM. Ask for Brochure mp/ 922 "Tax Rules for Children and Dependents."

NAIC (National Association of Investors Corporation)

P.O. Box 220

Royal Oak, MI 48068-0220

877-275-6242

www.better-investing.org

The National Council on Economic Education

1140 Avenue of the Americas

New York, NY 10036

212-730-7007

www.nationalcouncil.org

US Government Bonds

Bureau of the Public Debt

Savings Bonds

Parkersburg, WV 26106-1328

800-US-Bonds

US Mint

Office of Public Affairs

633 3rd Street, NW

Washington, DC 20220

202-874-6450

www.usmint.gov

Securities and Exchange Commission

Office of Investor Education

450 Fifth Street, NW

Washington, DC 20549

800-SEC-0330 or 202-942-7040

Index